25 TOP BLUES SONGS

TAB+ = TAB + TONE + TECHNIQUE

This is not your typical guitar tab book. In the new *Tab+* series from Hal Leonard, we provide you guidance on how to capture the guitar tones for each song as well as tips and advice on the techniques used to play the songs.

Where possible, we've confirmed the gear used on the original recordings via new and previously published interviews with the guitarists, producers, and/or engineers. Then we make general recommendations on how to achieve a similar tone, based on that info. You'll note that we do not mention specific modeling or software amps, as those units will typically contain models for the original amps we do cite.

Some of the songs herein will be easy to play even for advanced beginner players, whereas others present a much greater challenge. In either case, we've identified key techniques in each song that should help you learn the song with greater ease.

ISBN 978-1-4803-3026-9

HAL•LEONARD®
CORPORATION
7777 W. BLUEMOUND RD. P.O. BOX 13819 MILWAUKEE, WI 53213

Visit Hal Leonard Online at
www.halleonard.com

25 TOP BLUES SONGS

PERFORMANCE NOTES TAB. TONE. TECHNIQUE.
By Dave Rubin

ALBERT'S SHUFFLE
Mike Bloomfield

"Albert's Shuffle" is the lead track from *Super Session* (1968), an album Mike Bloomfield recorded with Stephen Stills and Al Kooper (the first of two he would record with Kooper). Having made a name for himself with the seminal Paul Butterfield Blues Band in the mid-sixties and backing Bob Dylan at his infamous performance at the Newport Folk Festival in 1965, as well as on his *Highway 61 Revisited*, Bloomfield became one of the first bonafide "guitar heroes." However, his restless nature and aversion to the illusory trappings of pop stardom would compel him to jump from project to project until his tragic and untimely death from an overdose in 1981. His exquisite phrasing, intense energy, and pure tone, however, had a profound effect on countless blues and rock guitarists who followed and remains just as revered today.

TONE
A 1959 sunburst Les Paul Standard, plugged straight into a cranked, pre-CBS Fender Twin Reverb, was all this blues god needed to make liquid gold flow from his fingers. In the studio, however, he most often played through a Fender Super Reverb (you can see one on the back of the LP cover) with the volume and treble on 10, reverb on 4, middle and bass barely up, and the bright switch on. Like B.B. King, one of his idols, Bloomfield usually had his pickup selector in the middle, with both P.A.F. 'buckers on, and would constantly fiddle with the volume and tone pots on his guitar to get the exact, fat "hi-fi" tone he desired.

To get your tone singing like "Bloomers," a humbucker-equipped Les Paul through a Fender combo (at least the size of a 20-watt Fender Deluxe Reverb) is your best option. However, you should be able to coax the sound out of a Gibson ES-335, SG—or even a humbucking PRS—through any high-quality Class A tube amp with at least one 12-inch speaker (e.g., Mesa Boogie).

TECHNIQUE
The medium-tempo, 12-bar instrumental blues "Albert's Shuffle" is a fitting tribute to Albert King and his classic, vocal-type string bending. That said, Bloomfield's sexy, "choked" notes and sensuous vibrato are a virtual tutorial in post-B.B. King blues guitar mastery. The pickup riff that extends across the bar line into measure 1 is "Electric Blues Guitar 101." Execute the bend on string 3 with the ring finger, followed by a small index-finger barre on strings 2–1, with the pinky—backed up by the ring, middle, and index fingers—pushing string 2 up to the root note. Note that Bloomfield maintained steady pressure against the frets when bending and vibratoing to achieve maximum natural sustain.

In an embarrassment of blues guitar riches, measure 6 of section letter E (the IV [C] chord) stands out as Bloomfield performs a "King's ransom" of bending techniques. Use the ring finger, backed by the middle and index, to access the one-step, one-and-a-half-step, and two-step bends on string 1. The classic double-string bend on strings 2–1 (beat 3) may be played à la Chuck Berry, pushing up with the ring finger as a small barre. An alternative is to place the middle finger on string 2 and the ring finger on string 1 and push up simultaneously. Observe that string 1's pitch is raised one-and-a-half steps, while string 2 goes up only one step due to the different distance each is squeezed.

ALL OF YOUR LOVE (ALL YOUR LOVE)
Magic Sam

Good things always come in threes, and blues guitar greats are no exception. Like the "Three Kings"—B.B., Albert, and Freddie—the "West Side of Chicago blues masters"—Otis Rush, Magic Sam, and Buddy Guy—came in triplicate. Sam Maghett followed hot on the heels of Otis Rush in 1957 with his own selection of certifiable classics for the indie Cobra Records, which was located on Chicago's west side. This tune was captured on tape in 1957 (included here) and again 10 years later—a slightly different version for *West Side Soul*. Though its minor key is emblematic of the sub-genre's sound, the impassioned performance and guitar style are all Sam. Tragically, he died of a heart attack in 1969 at the age of 32, just as he was crossing over, but his considerable influence remains undiminished.

TONE
Like his "blues brothers," Rush and Guy, Sam was attracted to the Strat, initially playing an early-fifties sunburst with a maple neck, while in the late sixties, he was seen with a 1965 transitional model with a rosewood fingerboard. It's unknown whether Sam recorded using an amp belonging to Cobra studios, or if he brought his own. The tremolo could indicate a 1955 Fender Tremolux, Gibson, or Ampeg, or a DeArmond outboard unit.

A Strat through a Deluxe Reverb, Super Reverb, or Twin Reverb with tremolo (erroneously called "vibrato" by Fender) will produce a version of the signature "watery" sound. Though Sam went straight into a fifties amp with raw, natural distortion, a Tube Screamer or similar stompbox can be used to approximate the tone with a newer amp. Use the bridge pickup on a Strat and adjust the volume pot accordingly.

TECHNIQUE

Like Freddie King, his Chicago blues peer, Sam was a spectacular trio guitarist. Though backed by the subtle piano of Little Brother Montgomery on this track, along with bass and drums, his skill of blending riffs, snappy fills, and vibrant ninth chords are on full display. The signature riff, first encountered in measures 1–2 of the intro, may be efficiently played with the ring, index, and ring fingers for the bass line, and the ring and index fingers barring at frets 9 and 7, respectively, for the harmonized minor triads. The subtle quarter-step, double-string bends in measures 1, 2, and 6 are best executed by pulling down with a small ring-finger barre. A similar technique should be applied to the bent triads in the guitar solo: push up with a ring-finger barre, a move that will require considerable pressure and strength.

BABY, SCRATCH MY BACK
Slim Harpo

The Stones and the Yardbirds, among other British Invasion bands, brought James "Slim Harpo" Moore and his appealing, accessible music to crossover prominence in the sixties with covers of his Louisiana swamp blues singles, including "I'm a King Bee" and "Got Love If You Want It." Slim's own recording of "Baby, Scratch My Back" hit #1 on the Billboard R&B charts as well as #16 on the Hot 100 charts in 1966, and gave his career a deserved boost. Although he regularly accompanied himself on guitar during live performances, in the Excello Records studio he was backed by his regular guitarists Rudolph "Rudy" Richard and James Johnson of the King Bees. Tragically, on the precipice of greater popularity via a tour of Europe, Slim died in London of a heart attack in 1970.

TONE

Slim is one of the few blues guitarists to favor the thin hollow body Gibson ES-330 with P-90 pickups as opposed to the more popular 335/45/55 semi-hollow series with humbuckers. It is unclear what gear Richard and Johnson played, though Johnson on lead guitar sounds like he may be picking a hollow body instrument. Verifying amps is always a tricky business as older blues guitarists often used whatever was available in the studio. The tremolo would suggest perhaps a pre-CBS blackface Fender or fifties to sixties Ampeg or Gibson amp. An ES-330, Epiphone Casino or similar thin hollow body with P-90 pickups through a 20–40 watt tube combo either containing built-in tremolo or with an outboard unit will produce the "swamp sound." Utilize the neck pickup and adjust the amp flat at 4–5 for treble, middle and bass.

TECHNIQUE

Slim is almost always shown in photos with a capo to facilitate ease of fingerings, but he only sings and blows harmonica on this track. Johnson is "stinging" the signature riffs and solo out of the root, extension, and root octave positions of the F composite blues scale, while Richard comps dominant barre chords. Access the major 3rd in the main riff by hammering on with the middle finger from the flat 3rd while barring at frets 1 (F), 6 (B♭) and 8 (C) for each chord change. One of several advantages to this approach is that it makes it possible to play instantly in other keys if desired by simply moving the pattern around the neck. Play the signature "chicken scratch" lick in section letter E with the index finger on the F note at fret 13 on string 1, while jabbing in a staccato fashion. Then bend the A♭ on fret 16 with the pinky backed by the ring, middle and index fingers.

BAD TO THE BONE
George Thorogood

George Thorogood, a serious semi-pro baseball player in his native Delaware in the '70s, once remarked that he would "rather be able to take the curve ball to right field than be a great guitarist." Though the former second baseman's ability to wait on the curve is unclear, he has used his limitations as a soloist to his advantage by reducing his chosen blues and fifties rock 'n' roll to the essentials: rhythm, riffs, and tone. In 1982, he released his best-known album, the gold-certified *Bad to the Bone*, which contained the title track, a song featuring his signature boogie blues. Thorogood claims that "Bad to the Bone" helped create the "classic rock" radio format when stations began playing it in the nineties. Still cranking strong as of 2014, Thorogood remains the unofficial king of the bar bands.

TONE

Like some of the greats he idolized, Thorogood was, for many years, identified with one guitar: a 1957–63 Gibson ES-125 TD with two P-90 pickups. He has owned several and at one point, painted them white for visual appeal, but any thin, hollow Gibson or Epiphone with P-90s will do the job. He appears to be unconcerned with what amps he uses in the studio, but is believed to have recorded through a silverface, post-CBS Fender Twin on his early albums. In concert, he would often play through a blackface Princeton Reverb miked through the PA system, though he has increased his horsepower over the years. On the smaller amps, he typically set the treble at 8, middle at 7, bass at 2.5, volume at 6.5, and reverb at 4, with the guitar's bridge pickup "floored." For his slides, Thorogood swears by "blue collar" copper pipe purchased from hardware stores, cut to length, and roughed up with sandpaper for a rawer sound.

TECHNIQUE

With a bone-crushing riff that's like a souped-up version of "Mannish Boy," Thorogood utilizes a handful of typical positions in open-G tuning, and wrings the blues out of them for all they're worth with a plastic thumbpick and bare fingers. In a manner similar to prewar bottleneck guitarists, he wears his slide on the pinky in order to free up the other three fingers for fretting and damping, as shown in measures 6–8 of the second guitar solo. Use the middle finger for the F and A notes on strings 6 and 5, respectively.

DOWN HOME BLUES
Z.Z. Hill

Flying under the radar of many northern and West Coast blues fans in the eighties was southern soul-blues singer Arzell "Z.Z." Hill and his equally overlooked Jackson, Mississippi label, Malaco Records. Hill had been performing professionally since the mid-sixties, and together, they appealed to a more mature African-American audience looking for meaningful songs instead of instrumental flash. Released in 1982, *Down Home* was embedded in the charts for two years. In addition, the single "Down Home Blues" reportedly went gold and is considered the most famous blues tune of the decade, a striking accomplishment for a rather basic 12-bar shuffle. Unfortunately, Hill died of a heart attack in 1984 following an accident.

TONE

Unsung southern blues guitar hero Leroy Emmanuel plays the signature riffs in the verses, the fills in the choruses, and the guitar solo. He shoulders a Gibson ES-335 with a trapeze tailpiece, with both 'buckers selected and likely through a CBS-era (or later) Fender Twin. His usage of bare fingers, the short sustain of the non-stop tailpiece, and the moderate amp volume make for a relatively delicate, refined sound that compliments the smooth, nuanced vibe of the tune.

TECHNIQUE

Emmanuel (Gtr. 1) fashions his verse 1 accompaniment with a classic chordal riff that implies IV–I harmony relative to the I (G7) and IV (C7) chord changes. Barre the IV chord with the ring finger, barre two frets lower with the index, and hammer on with the middle finger. The V (D7) and IV changes in measures 9–10 of each verse are formed entirely from the specific harmony, and the fingering involves the index as a barre, the middle finger to hammer, and the thumb employed for the root bass note on string 6. In verse 2, he intelligently combines elements from the two main patterns from verse 1. Building subtle momentum, in measures 1–4 of chorus 1, Emmanuel embellishes the riff from verse 1 with minor pentatonic licks that involve bending from C to D on string 3 with the ring finger.

Check out the cool, deceptively simple bass-string lick in measure 12 of verse 3. Bend the F on string 4 a quarter step by pushing up with the index finger. Next, quickly slide the index finger to the C note on string 5 and access the C♯ and D notes with the middle and ring fingers, respectively. In addition, be sure to observe the slinky double-string bends in measure 8 of the chorus that precedes the outro-chorus. Pull down with the ring finger at fret 5, and the index finger at fret 3 on strings 3–2, keeping in mind that the pitches notated are approximate, with the bends creating a bluesy effect rather than exact scale tones.

FIRST TIME I MET THE BLUES
Buddy Guy

Buddy Guy was the third of the "Big Three" West Side blues guitar pioneers. While serving as "house guitarist" at Chess Records in the early sixties, Guy was also afforded the opportunity to cut singles under his own name. "First Time I Met the Blues" (1960) shows his unfiltered passion, though he was only three years removed from his home in Louisiana and still exhibiting a sizeable debt to B.B. King. The fact was not lost on Leonard Chess, who was reluctant to promote him, though he would come to regret it later when he heard the loud blues that Guy was performing in the clubs in the late sixties. In time, Guy would go on to achieve tremendous renown, influencing a slew of heavyweight electric blues and blues-rock guitarists, including Jimi Hendrix, Eric Clapton and Stevie Ray Vaughan, among many others. In the nineties, after a shamefully extended period of being unsigned, he experienced a comeback and the delayed success that continues unabated today.

TONE

In the early fifties, Ike Turner became one of the earliest blues cats to manhandle a Strat, and Buddy Holly looked smart strumming his '58 sunburst on the *Ed Sullivan Show*. After Otis Rush, Buddy Guy was one of the first Chicago bluesman to make the Strat his iconic instrument when he bought a brand new '57 sunburst model with a maple fretboard. His amp of choice would become a late-fifties Fender Bassman, a musical marriage many consider to be the ultimate blues machine. However, in 1960, he was not allowed to push the volume and exploit the thick, rich, overdriven sound capabilities inherent in the magical combination. Nonetheless, while playing on the bridge pickup, he created enough bite to express his explosive passion.

A whammy-bar-equipped Stratocaster of virtually any vintage, set on the bridge pickup and played through a medium-sized tube combo of 20 to 40 watts—with moderate gain; the bass, middle, and treble at 5–6, and reverb at 4—should provide a reasonable facsimile of his early, classic, unadulterated tone.

TECHNIQUE
In the mid-fifties, Ike Turner went stone crazy with the whammy bar on his Strat with his Kings of Rhythm band, and he likely passed the technique onto Buddy Guy, who backed him on "This is the End" and "You Sure Can't Do" in 1958. Both Strat-masters used the bar to execute mostly fast, aggressive vibrato and the occasional dip, as shown in measure 4 of verse 1, though Guy rarely—if ever—touches the bar today. In measure 7 of verse 1, measures 1, 5, 7, and 9 of verse 2, and measure 1 of verse 3, Guy repeats a tangy motif over the I, IV, and V chords that involves a one-step, double-string whammy bar bend and fierce vibrato that should be performed with the ring and pinky fingers, low to high. Have no fear about being too rambunctious or breaking strings by yanking up on the bar like you are ripping pull tabs off cold brews!

GOING DOWN
Freddie King
Chronologically, the third of the legendary "Kings of the blues," Freddie King was arguably the most talented. In addition to being a virtuoso and one of the greatest trio guitarists of all time, he produced a career's worth of original, classic instrumentals, along with as many exceptional vocal tunes. After his remarkably productive run of unparalleled blues creativity with King/Federal Records ended in 1966, he tread water with Atlantic/Cotillion until signing with Leon Russell's Shelter Records in 1969. His first of three albums with Russell, *Getting Ready*, was recorded at the old Chess Studio in Chicago and released in 1971, featuring the Don Nix blues-rocker "Going Down." The song signaled a distinct change of direction for the "Texas Cannonball," one that would help him crossover to the rock audience that would sustain him until his untimely death in 1976 from alcohol-abuse complications. He was just 42 years old. Like B.B. and Albert, his influence and importance to electric blues and rock cannot be overstated.

TONE
After playing a 1956 Les Paul Goldtop with P-90 pickups, and later, a 1963 Gibson ES-345, by the seventies, King had moved on to a cherry-red Gibson ES-355 with a Lyre vibrola (that he never used). In the studio, he may have been abusing the speakers of a Fender Twin, Super Reverb, or a Gibson Stereo CA79. In concert, he was seen and heard frying the tubes of a Fender Quad Reverb, with the volume and treble at 10 and the other EQ at 0. The combination of his plastic thumbpick, metal index-finger pick, as well as the varitone setting on his 355, produced a top end that could be near lethal. Photos from the era suggest he usually selected both humbuckers and had the varitone in the first, or "no cut," position, resulting in a sound with both bite and depth. Be aware that having both pickups engaged allows for a variety of sounds by blending different volumes and tones. A 335 or similar semi-hollowbody set on the bridge 'bucker through a 50–100 watt tube combo with the "Freddie King settings" should approximate the sound on "Going Down."

TECHNIQUE
Though not notated, playing the chords with staccato 16th notes and all downstrokes in sync with the bass (Duck Dunn on the record) is recommended. And, while even a seasoned professional may find it exhausting and taxing on the strumming hand, keeping the power surging nonstop is worth the effort.

King possessed the ability to apply a brutal attack on his strings for breathtaking dynamics. His method included utilizing the metal fingerpick on his index like a claw by snapping *up* on the strings, though a heavy flat pick should produce a similar result. The fury with which he pummeled the strings with his left hand translated into aggressive bending and lightning-fast vibrato, intensified by shaking the strings, as well as the neck of his 355, with a vengeance.

I AIN'T DRUNK
Albert Collins
The revered "Master of the Telecaster" experienced an arc to his career similar to Freddie King. Relative success with a string of instrumentals in the late fifties was followed by almost two decades of scuffling between small record companies, despite the enthusiastic support of Canned Heat's Bob "Bear" Hite and pop singer Neil Diamond. Fortuitously, in 1978, Collins signed with Chicago's Alligator Records, introducing him to a much larger audience, and this final, "third act" was his most productive and rewarding. "I Ain't Drunk" appeared on *Cold Snap* (1983), his seventh release for the premier blues label featuring his old buddy, B-3 organist Jimmy McGriff, and was a contemporary take on the classic organ groups from back in the day.

TONE
A 1961 Tele with a humbucking pickup in the neck position, cutting like an ice pick in conjunction with a 1972 Fender Quad Reverb (volume, treble, and middle on 10; reverb on 4; and bass on 0), is the razor-sharp sound heard on the recording and by audiences in concert. Rounding out the potentially deafening high frequencies was his practice of blending the

'bucker and the bridge position single-coil pickup, as well as his utilization of bare fingers for picking, plucking, and snapping the strings. His powerful creation was an instantly recognizable sound—steely bright, yet "squawking" with rich mid and upper overtones—that stood out from the multitude of other Tele players. Although referred to as the "cool sound," it was actually more like fire and brimstone.

TECHNIQUE

Like Albert King, Collins employed a unique altered tuning—essentially F minor (F–C–F–A♭–C–F, low to high)—to facilitate his distinct, personal style of playing. The tuning, combined with a capo, enabled Collins to play in open position at all times, with root octaves quickly available and the ability to easily access the major 3rd on string 3 by hammering on one fret above the capo.

"I Ain't Drunk" contains a couple of Collins' "cool" signature licks that may be performed in standard tuning, particularly if the index finger is used as a barre at fret 4. In measures 17–20, Gtr. 1 (Collins) plays a repetitive lick containing a tonality-defining dyad with a hammer-on that requires a challenging stretch in standard tuning. Anchor the ring finger at fret 4 of string 1 ("0" in tab) and hammer from fret 3 to fret 6 of string 3 with your index and pinky, respectively, plucking string 3 with the thumb and string 1 with the index finger.

In measure 1 of the outro-guitar solo, Collins executes one of his classic pull-off patterns. Barre strings 3–1 at fret 4 ("0" in tab) and, on beat 1, pull off on string 2 with the pinky and ring fingers. On beat 2, pull off with the ring finger. On beat 3, pull off with the pinky and ring fingers. In measure 17, again, barre strings 3–1 at fret 4 ("0" in tab) and pluck strings 3 and 1 simultaneously with the thumb and index finger, respectively. On string 1, access fret 3 with the ring finger and fret 5 with the pinky.

I SMELL SMOKE
Michael Burks

Michael "Iron Man" Burks was one of those blazing entities who rarely come around. Like actual celestial bodies, they burn bright in the firmament and then disappear. Following his impressive indie debut in 1999, the seemingly indestructible, powerhouse performer signed with Chicago's Alligator Records in 2001. *I Smell Smoke* was his second release for the premier blues label, and the title track was aptly named, as it emanated odiferous funk and molten heat. He would live to see only one more record release in his lifetime, resulting in a short but lasting legacy.

TONE

The influence of Albert King loomed large in Burks' playing, as well as his mellifluous vocals. Indeed, embracing the comparison, he was known for slinging a Gibson Flying V and his tone on "I Smell Smoke" has the "flute-like" sound in the upper register and sustain similar to King Albert. Contrary to most blues cats, Burks enthusiastically utilized a variety of gear to get his smokin' tone. He favored muscular amps, and his rig during this period consisted of a custom Dumble, a Dr. Z Delta 88, and a Dr. Z Mazerati Sr., along with a pedalboard containing a Klon Centaur, a custom-made Teese Wheels of Fire wah, and a Boss delay. His settings tended to feature the bass and mids full up and the treble cut. Burks' main guitar was an eighties Gibson Flying V ("The V") with EMG 85 pickups and an SPC control, though he would also trade off to historic Les Pauls and a late-model Strat.

Gibson humbucking pickups (or hot replacements) in a solidbody guitar and a high-gain tube amp of 50 watts or more are required to begin building the "Iron Man" tone. In addition, a high-end, high-gain overdrive/distortion pedal like the Klon Centaur should enhance the natural guitar and amp sound, rather than coloring it. Boost the bass and midrange while leaving the treble low on the amp, and play full volume on the bridge pickup for a wilder "woman tone."

TECHNIQUE

Burks bends and vibratos with extreme passion, which wells up from his soul and explodes through his fingers. Whether on the B♭ at fret 18 of string 1 (measures 5–6 of the intro) or the B♭ at fret 15 of string 3 (measures 5 and 8 of verse 1), use the ring finger, backed by the middle and index. Besides offering increased strength and control, this approach will place your hand in an advantageous position to access with the index finger the critical A♭ *blues* note two frets below on either string. At the same time, observe the efficient hand position relative to pushing up the quarter-step bend from A♭ to the "true" blue note with the index finger in measure 4 of the intro and measure 8 of the guitar solo.

I'M YOURS AND I'M HERS
Johnny Winter

The legend of the blindingly white guy who could play blindingly fast blues guitar germinated in Texas even before he was brought to New York and signed a record-setting contract with Columbia Records in 1968. *The Progressive Blues Experiment*, a tepid collection of (mostly) standards recorded in Austin before his discovery, was rush-released first, but his next album *Johnny Winter* was the paradigm changer, taking off with the original, amped-up country blues of "I'm Yours and I'm Hers." In the seventies, following the addition of butt-kicking *"rock and roll!!!"* into his steaming blues stew, Winter became the biggest arena rock star of the decade and still gigs to the delight of his legions of fans.

TONE
Despite his ongoing flirtation with the headless Lazer guitar, Winter will always be known for his vintage reverse Firebirds, especially his iconic 1963 sunburst Firebird III. However, for his debut and a couple of years thereafter, he relied on a 1966 Fender XII solidbody electric with split single-coil pickups, similar to the Precision Bass, but refitted for six strings. A preferred amp was a pre-CBS Fender Super Reverb. He has always favored a bright, biting sound with the treble, mids and volume cranked, but with zero bass and the reverb around 4 or slightly above. Though skewed towards the higher frequencies, his sound is meaty, not thin, likely due to playing on both pickups, as opposed to the bridge pickup only.

Given the rarity of the Fender XII (the original issue was discontinued after 1969), Winter's initial signature tone can be achieved with a Strat or Tele through a 40–50 watt tube amp with two 12-inch or four 10-inch speakers and adjusted to his settings. The middle pickup on the former axe or the middle selector position on the latter, plugged straight into the amp with the volume nearly pegged, should provide the desired whiny growl while retaining the "beef."

TECHNIQUE
Winter's tribute to Robert Johnson, and specifically "Cross Road Blues," contains the Texas guitar slinger playing a slashing slide part in open-A tuning (Gtr. 2) and a sinewy fretted part (Gtr. 1). Wear the slide on your pinky finger, like Winter and the prewar country bluesmen he idolized. He is partial to a homemade metal slide cut from a hi-hat stand (now available in a mass-produced version), but any brass or steel slide that fits snugly, yet comfortably, will suffice. Winter uses a combination of plastic thumbpick and his index and middle fingers for both parts, as well. When playing slide, muting unwanted string noise with both the left and the right hand is imperative. With the former, clamp the index, middle, and ring fingers together like a four-finger barre and drag them lightly over the strings, behind the slide, being careful not to press them down to the frets.

Gtr. 1 features numerous bends up and down the fingerboard and on all strings, as has always been his practice, but be aware that Winter consistently bends with his ring finger (as does Clapton and others), instead of utilizing his pinky, backed by the other fingers. While it is a minor point of contention, some guitarists feel that compared with the pinky, the ring finger achieves a more robust sound, especially on strings 1–2. Nonetheless, the ring finger sometimes does require hand repositioning where the pinky would be more efficient. An exception clearly occurs in measure 7 of the guitar solo, however, where the B note on string 2 should be bent with the ring finger, backed by the middle and index, while the pinky accesses the E on string 1.

IT HURT SO BAD
Susan Tedeschi
Though the title may have meant to imply her resolve and artistic indestructibility, on *Just Won't Burn* (1998), Boston native Susan Tedeschi sparked, smoldered, and flat-out seared an unsuspecting blues world with incendiary vocals and raw passion unheard since Janis Joplin. The album went gold and hit #2 on the Top Blues Albums chart. A fine, tasteful if modest player in her own right, Tedeschi often deferred to her young, firebrand lead guitarist, Sean Costello, who is featured and showed hip R&B chops on "It Hurt So Bad."

TONE
Costello was known for his 1953 Gibson Gold Top with P-90 pickups and "wrap-tail" bridge, as well as a 1997 LP Gold Top R6 reissue. Anyone who thinks humbuckers, either P.A.F. or patent, are the only way to go needs to play an LP or ES-330 with P-90s! Bite, gobs of tone, and power! Costello used a variety of Fender combo amps, including a blackface Deluxe Reverb, a blackface Vibrolux, and a blackface Pro Reverb, and he achieved his "syrupy" tone the old-fashioned way—plugging straight into the amp.

As opposed to other guitar/pickup combinations, there is no reasonable facsimile for a P-90. In addition to various LP models and the 330, P-90 powered SGs and Epiphones are available too, and could go straight into a 20–50 watt tube combo. With the neck pickup (or both) on, set the treble at 6, mid at 4, bass at 5, reverb at 4, and control volume from the guitar.

TECHNIQUE
One of the cool parts of this eight-bar R&B ballad "It Hurt So Bad" is the chord melody and harmonized fills performed by Costello in the verses and guitar solo. The signature 3rds motif in measure 1 of the intro and measure 7 of the verse should be played with the middle and index fingers for the span of one fret, and with the ring and index fingers for the span of two frets. The fills embellishing the A7 and E7 changes are typical of the genre and easily accessed by barring with the index finger at frets 7 and 9, respectively, and hammering on with the ring finger.

The guitar solo, which actually begins in measure 8 of the third verse, is an R&B tour de force of choice blues licks, 3rds, and 6ths by Costello. A veritable textbook for guitarists, it would be wise to study and analyze this solo measure by measure. Dig how he begins by engaging in dynamic "call and response" via single-note lines from the A composite blues scale, plus hammered 3rds and sliding 6ths in an embarrassment of melodic and harmonic riches. Measures 4–5 are especially brilliant, as he seamlessly and dramatically connects the sweet, singing notes in measure 4 to the gritty blues "train whistle" in measure 5. Play the former by starting with a combination of the index and ring fingers until beat 3. Use the index finger for the B note at fret 7 of string 1 and the pinky for the A note at fret 10 of string 2. This fingering will place the hand in an advantageous position for an efficient transition to the G-note bend at fret 8 of string 2 (the index finger remains on the B note). After building a head of steam, Costello hits his climax in measure 7, where throbbing 6ths at fret 17 imply A7 to D9, fingered with the middle and index and middle and ring, respectively.

LAUNDROMAT
Rory Gallagher

Like his fellow countryman Van Morrison, Rory Gallagher was a "tortured" Irish soul drawn naturally to the blues. A supremely gifted instrumentalist, singer, and songwriter, he first displayed his talents, including on alto sax and harmonica, in the blues-rock and jazzy power trio Taste from 1966–70. He released his self-titled solo debut in 1971. Save for a cover of Muddy's "Gypsy Woman," the album contained all originals, including "Laundromat," and Gallagher would go on to have a long, productive, and much-admired recording and performing career. Tragically, he died in 1995 from complications following a liver transplant.

TONE
Although many famed blues guitarists have been identified with one specific guitar model, Gallagher played one *specific guitar* since 1963, when he purchased a 1961 sunburst Fender Strat with rosewood fingerboard, reportedly the first one to arrive in Ireland. The Strat would be his pride and joy till the end of his life and was only out of his hands for a short period, when it was stolen and later found in a rainy ditch. Over time, it would acquire great character through severe finish wear while undergoing hardware replacements, including the pickups. In the early '70s, he used it to overheat the tubes in a VOX AC-30 Top Boost amp with the help of a Dallas Rangemaster Treble Booster pedal—the same kind employed by Eric Clapton on the "Beano" Bluesbreakers album. Videos from the era show Gallagher playing the signature riffs and comp chords on the bridge pickup and the solo on the neck pickup. On the studio recording, however, it sounds like he remains on the bridge pickup, but steps on the Rangemaster for some extra "buzz." His amp settings sound mostly flat, with the bass cut. In 2011, Gallagher's brother, Donal, allowed Joe Bonamassa to play the Strat for two nights at the London Hammersmith Apollo.

TECHNIQUE
The signature riff is a unique, creative take on the boogie beat and cunningly simple. The "trick" is to fret carefully in order to include the open strings. This requires observing when to use just the tip of the index and ring fingers (beats 2–3 in measure 1 of the intro) and when to barre with the index finger (measure 4; at fret 5, combined with pulling down a quarter step) or the ring finger (measure 2; at fret 7).

Measures 9–12 of the guitar solo contain a surprising sequence for a blues tune; it's startling to hear on the recording, as if a second guitarist has suddenly entered the picture to play harmony with Gallagher, though actually easy to reproduce. Use only the index finger to play the A Mixolydian mode notes on string 5 in conjunction with the open fifth string, hammering from C♯ to D with the middle finger in measure 11 and from D to E with the ring finger in measure 12.

LAUNDROMAT BLUES
Albert King

King Albert was the "King String Bender" and arguably the most influential electric blues guitarist in the sixties following his signing with Stax Records in 1966, with Jimi Hendrix, Mike Bloomfield, Eric Clapton, and Stevie Ray Vaughan being some of his most famous acolytes. "Laundromat Blues" is one of eleven classic tracks on the epochal *Born Under a Bad Sign* (1967) that changed the game forever. Backed by Booker T. & the MG's, the magical and near-mythical combination of the funky, soulful Stax house band and the big string-strangler established the benchmark for contemporary blues guitar and is just as vital today as it was over 40 years ago. When King died of a heart attack in 1992, an irreplaceable giant of postwar blues left a huge void in the firmament. As Joe Walsh memorably said, "Albert King could blow away most contemporary guitarists with his standby switch on."

TONE
Virtually every great blues guitarist—from B.B. King, with his semi-hollow ES-355s ("Lucille"), to SRV, with his pre-CBS Strats—has wielded an iconic model. To go with his extra-large size and outsized personality, Albert King swung perhaps the most attention-getting axe of all: a 1958 Gibson Flying V that he supposedly bought new. Though known for playing a 1967 solid-state Acoustic 260 bass head on top of a 261 cabinet with two 15-inch Altec speakers in the late sixties and

seventies, King likely recorded "Laundromat Blues" and other singles from that era through a 1960–64, 40-watt, brown Tolex, brownface Fender Concert amp with four 10-inch speakers that was owned by the Stax studio.

Be aware that significant elements of his sound came from his idiosyncratic tuning (see Technique) and from picking with his bare thumb. Nonetheless, playing a solidbody, dual-humbucker Gibson with both pickups on and their volumes around 4 or 5, the tone on the neck pickup wide open, and the tone on the bridge pickup rolled off, would be a start. A 40–50 watt tube combo with two 12-inch, or better yet, four 10-inch speakers, with the volume wide open, the treble at 5, middle at 4, bass at 6, and little or no reverb, should complete the A.K. alchemy.

TECHNIQUE
Questions about Albert King's tuning continue long after his passing. Steve Cropper surreptitiously observed it in the studio as being, low to high, C–B–E–F♯–B–E. In 1989, luthier Dan Erlewine noted it as C–F–C–F–A–D, strung with .050, .038, .028, .024w, .012, and .009 strings. This writer was told by Little Jimmie King, who backed Big Albert for four years, that the tuning was "F," apparently lending credence to the Erlewine discovery. However, based on evidence from numerous live performance videos, we at Hal Leonard believe it to be B–E–B–E–G♯–C♯, which is a variation of open-G tuning (D–G–D–G–B–D) tuned down one-and-a-half steps, but with string 1 starting at standard pitch (E) before being detuned. Though it is not necessary to duplicate his tuning to play like King, you should be aware that the decrease in string tension made string bending easier for the "Velvet Bulldozer," whether he needed it or not. In addition, due to his playing a right-handed V upside down, he pulled down rather than pushing up to achieve his multi-step bends and shimmying vibrato.

The double-string bends in measures 1–3 and 5 of the guitar solo are signature licks of the big fellow and may best be executed by us mere mortals by catching both strings under the ring finger, backed by the middle and index, and pushing up.

LONG DISTANCE BLUES
Joe Bonamassa
To describe Joe Bonamassa as a "child prodigy" is like calling Michael Jordan a "basketball player"; the faint praise diminishes them. Bonamassa was learning Stevie Ray Vaughan licks at 7, was tutored by virtuoso Danny Gatton at 11, and by 14, was in a band called Bloodlines with Berry Oakley Jr, Erin Davis (son of Miles), and Waylon Krieger (son of Robby). "Long Distance Blues," from *Blues Deluxe*, his third solo release with a varied selection of mostly covers, shows his unabashed and unapologetic admiration for British blues and Jeff Beck in particular. "When I heard Rod Stewart and the Jeff Beck Group singing 'Let Me Love You, Baby' [from *Truth*], it changed my life. I knew exactly what I wanted to do," the guitarist enthuses. Bonamassa has gone on to ignore the "blues police" and play the blues *his* way, with an explosive combination of energy and deep, blues emotion.

TONE
Bonamassa has earned the honor of having his name added to the list of loyal, illustrious Les Paul players with signature models. However, on "Long Distance Blues," he appears to be using an ES-335 through two different amps and a Fender reverb tank: likely a Budda Superdrive 30 for the "clean" intro and verses and a Marshall Silver Jubilee 2555 blended with the Budda for the hair-singeing guitar solo. The Buddxa's EQ settings appear to be around 5 with the volume up and his guitar volume down on the bridge humbucker for a noticeable dollop of natural distortion, while the Marshall settings tend to be high treble, moderate midrange, and heavy bass, also with the volume slanted towards the upper end and rolled up from the guitar for maximum dynamic effect.

Curiously, when Bonamassa cranks his axe through the Marshall, he sounds an awful lot like Clapton on the "Beano" Bluesbreakers album. Consequently, a 'bucker-powered Gibson on the bridge pickup through a Fender Deluxe Reverb or similar small tube combo with the volume at 8, treble at 4–5, the bass up, and reverb on 4 for the clean sound and a 45-watt Marshall combo set like the Jubilee for the solo, could do the trick. Or, a perfectly acceptable sound can be achieved with one amp, perhaps a Bassman or Twin, driven by a real tube stompbox like a Kingsley Jester, BK Tube Driver, Effectrode Tube Drive or an old Ibanez Tube King.

TECHNIQUE
Bonamassa reveals no surprises in his choice of scales in the guitar solo, relying on the ubiquitous minor pentatonic in G. In addition to superior chops and impeccable phrasing, his choice of scale positions lend distinction, as well. In measure 5, over the IV (C) chord, he pummels probably the least used position (at fret 12). Try it with the pinky and middle fingers on frets 15 and 13 of string 1, respectively, and the pinky and index fingers on frets 15 and 12 of string 2, respectively. Observe that the same, repetitive four-note pattern could be more easily accessed around fret 8 of string 1, with the ring and index fingers at frets 10 and 8, respectively, and, on string 2, with the pinky and index fingers at frets 11 and 8, respectively.

The blistering G7 triple stop over the IV chord in measure 67 should be played, low to high, with the index, ring and middle fingers, while the thirty-second notes are ripped with blurred alternate down- and upstrokes.

MAMA TALK TO YOUR DAUGHTER

Robben Ford

Robben Ford's journey to the "real" blues was circuitous, with the alto saxophone being his first instrument, followed by the guitar and concurrent with an interest in jazz and the blues he heard in the '60s. Productive time spent in blues, jazz, and fusion groups would finally lead to *Talk to Your Daughter*, a full-fledged blues album of mostly classic covers featuring his simultaneously sophisticated and passionate guitar playing, along with his melodious blues vocals. The J.B. Lenoir title track swings like mad and is regularly lauded as a benchmark for sumptuous, silky-smooth tone.

TONE

Ford has utilized a number of very different guitars over the years and, like other great masters of the silver strings, tends to sound the same on each, especially from the '80s forward. In 1988, he was seen playing a custom Sakashta Noupaul guitar with humbuckers live, but word is that he played a variety of Fenders on the Grammy-nominated *Talk to Your Daughter* album, and the title track certainly sounds like a single-coil bridge pickup. His later love affair with a certain 1960 Telecaster would seem to support the theory. Legendary boutique amp builder Paul Rivera claims Ford used one of his custom Rivera M-100 amps with four 10-inch speakers on "Talk to Your Daughter," not the 1982 Dumble (#102) Ford was favoring at that moment and continued to use thereafter. There was a time after the recording when Ford was fond of using a Hermida Technology Zendrive Boost, a TC Electronics 2290 Delay, and a Lexicon reverb. More recently, he has greatly simplified his set-up and has been playing rental Twins on the road.

Without resorting to the cliché that it's "all in the fingers"—though his employment of bare right-hand fingers does contribute to the warmth of his tone—quality, single-coil Fender guitars or Gibson guitars with classic P-90 pickups is the place to start for the Robben Ford mojo. His hallmark is a fat, open sound with little-to-no obvious compression, and he has stated that a Twin would be his second choice after the Dumble. Hence, a muscular, 80–100 watt tube amp with the master volume at 5 or above (and the gain channels, if available, set low), treble at 6, midrange at 4, bass at 6, and reverb at 5 will provide a big, rich tone with a hint of natural harmonic distortion from the power tubes, rather than from the preamp. A solidbody guitar with the selector on the single-coil bridge pickup and the volume at 8, plus a quality overdrive/distortion box such as the Zendrive, adjusted accordingly, should supply the desired polished sustain.

TECHNIQUE

Ford swings with exquisite precision, and the primary goal while performing the fills and guitar solo in "Talk to Your Daughter" should be the same. The repetitive, descending double-stop pattern in measures 13–15 is a blues classic that adds a welcome dash of harmony, as well as momentum, to the I (G) chord. Use the ring/middle (low to high), the index as a small barre, and the middle/index (low to high). A characteristic of great blues and blues-influenced guitarists is the way they interpret clichés to make them fresh and expressive. Following the double stops, Ford leads into verse 1 with a classic "Albert King box" lick (measure 16) at moderate volume and with a light touch, embellished handsomely with two quick hammer-ons to the root (G) note. Gliss back and forth between F and G on string 2 with the index finger, hitting the D note on string 3 with the middle finger and hammering with gusto from F to G with the index and ring fingers. Consequently, the ring finger is employed to sustain and vibrato the root for three long, sinuous beats in measure 1 of verse 1, demonstrating consummate fluidity. In measures 7–9 of the second verse, Ford demonstrates the power of dynamics by digging in hard with his left hand and with the pick. In measure 7, bend the C note on string 3 a full step to D with the ring finger, backed by the middle and index fingers, and allow it to grind against the F, which is accessed by the pinky. With haste, bend the C note a half step with the already-engaged ring finger. In measures 8–9, continue down the root position of the G minor pentatonic scale with a combination of the index and ring fingers, resolving to the root (D) note at fret 17 of string 5 with the ring finger.

NO, NO BABY

Son Seals

Following the unprecedented blues revival in the sixties, a musical "hangover" of sorts occurred in the blues world in the early seventies. Fortunately for fans, in 1976, former Albert King drummer and contemporary Chicago blues guitarist Son "Bad Axe" Seals broke free from the torpor with the blazing *Midnight Son*. His second release, the album drives hard with a kicking horn section adding to Son's aggressive, staccato attack and his chesty, growling vocals. "No, No Baby" is one of nine originals and a hefty chunk of funk, with syncopation intensified by dramatic stop-time.

TONE

Though Seals is shown with a thin Japanese hollowbody guitar on the album cover, a 1967–73 semi-hollow Guild Starfire V with humbucking pickups through a 1955–60 tweed 4x10 Fender Bassman were the expressive musical tools of his sound. The resultant "barroom" tone is one of the great signature sounds of the blues: thick and harmonically rich, with a fierce roar to match his voice.

Though acknowledged by the cognoscenti as perhaps the ultimate blues guitar amp, a vintage Bassman or reissue can be quite pricey. Some alternatives could be a 40-watt Fender Blues Deluxe reissue, a 12-watt Fender '57 Deluxe reissue, or a similar tweed-style amp from other manufacturers. Be aware that vintage 40-watt blackface Super Reverbs with four 10-inch speakers have much different circuitry, and even when cranked, will not sound like a Bassman or other classic tweed amps.

A Gibson ES-335 will suffice as a stand-in for a Starfire and is, in fact, what Seals later played. Use both pickups or just the bridge pickup, with the amp "dimed" on volume, treble, midrange (if available), and bass (no reverb, and definitely no stompboxes, please!). Control the amount of drive and volume from the guitar.

TECHNIQUE

The "secret" to playing like Seals may be answered in one sentence: Pick virtually every note hard, with mostly downstrokes.

RECONSIDER BABY

Eric Clapton

Clapton's fans on the London blues scene in 1965 were so worshipful during his tenure with John Mayall's Bluesbreakers that "Clapton is God" was seen scrawled on an Underground station wall. But, despite being hailed as a bluesman of uncommon ability and artistic expression, he wavered in the succeeding decades between being the "man of the blues," in Chuck Berry's memorable accolade, and the glamorous rock guitar hero. Indeed, not until 1994 did he finally commit to recording *From the Cradle*, a true blues album consisting of accurate reproductions of classics near and dear to his heart. "Reconsider, Baby," as made famous by Lowell Fulson in 1953, is faithful to a fault to the original, save for the solos by old "Slowhand," which are delivered with both respect and additional energy.

TONE

Clapton reportedly used as many as 50 guitars to record *From the Cradle*, with an early-sixties ES-335 crackling through a modified 1957 tweed Fender Twin to provide the vintage vibe for "Reconsider, Baby." Though not the big, "woody" tone that Lowell Fulson achieved with his fat, hollow Gibson ES-5, Clapton's tone is redolent in natural overtones nonetheless.

Any quality semi-hollow such as an ES-335 or Epiphone Riviera, or a thin hollowbody guitar like a Gibson ES-330 or an Epiphone Casino set on the bridge pickup and run through a tweed Fender with the treble at 7 and bass boosted, will work just dandy. A budget alternative would be a good tube amp of 20–50 watts with a TS-7, TS-8, or TS-9 Tube Screamer.

TECHNIQUE

In measures 3–5 of the intro, execute the classic, signature glisses with the index finger. In measure 9, play the Bb/E dyad with the ring and pinky fingers in order to leave your hand in an advantageous location to continue riffing in the root position of the blues scale with the addition of the major 3rd (B) from the Mixolydian mode (fret 4 of string 3 and fret 2 of string 5). Access the B note on string 3 by glissing into it from Bb (the flat 3rd) with the index finger, using the same approach in the verses and guitar solo.

Ultimately, the "cream" of Clapton is his phrasing, the most esoteric element of soloing to teach, worthy of a book or more unto itself. However, try taking a deep breath before each lick and then let it out as you play. Pause as you take your next breath and repeat the process. Yes, it does make it difficult to do on the longer lines, but it is recommended in order to get the proper flow of notes.

RIGHT NEXT DOOR

Robert Cray

Though Stevie Ray Vaughan rightfully receives the lion's share of the credit for initiating the second "blues revival" in the eighties, blues and soul man Robert Cray deserves acknowledgment, too. His fifth studio album, *Strong Persuader*, went double platinum and pushed his crossover appeal over the top. "Right Next Door," totally emblematic of his style, is a unique combination of classy rhythm guitar and a succinct solo, with the underlying depth of the blues supporting Cray's favorite lyric content, the illicit affair.

TONE

The surprise is not that Cray is a "Strat man," but that he has created, absent any outboard effects, his own "clean" signature sound, emphasizing his exceptionally expressive and dynamic left and right hand touch in a manner somewhat reminiscent of Mark Knopfler in early Dire Straits. The owner of a stable of Leo Fender's proudest achievement, he plays a '57 sunburst Strat (maple board, of course) strung with hefty .011, .013, .018, .028, .036, and .046 gauge strings, with the selector switch set in the notch between the neck and middle pickups.

A Fender Super Reverb and Twin Reverb in tandem, with the volume at 5, treble at 10, midrange at 10, bass at 4, and reverb on 3, and the guitar volume at 7–8, produces his refined tone. While a 40–100 watt Fender tube combo should be the first choice, another, comparable brand will work with a Strat.

TECHNIQUE
Leave it to the intelligent and knowledgeable Cray to know a hip chord like the Cm11 in the intro. Though it may be a literal stretch to access, it sets the tune's ambience and is absolutely required in the performance. Barre across fret 1 with the index finger and apply the middle, ring, and pinky fingers, low to high. Be aware how his sophisticated rhythm guitar playing is the heart and soul of the song, predicated on a variety of techniques, including left- and right-hand muting and subtly propulsive strumming that incorporates syncopated down- and upstrokes, as well as delicate broken chords in the pre-chorus. Cray keeps his right-hand fingers lightly clenched as his hand floats above the pick guard, resulting in snappy pick strokes.

Dig the "squawky" tone in the guitar solo, achieved by "red lining" the Strat volume, and also note how Cray finds a home in the upper extension of the C minor pentatonic scale, affectionately known as the "Albert King box." Execute the classic one-step bends on string 1 with the ring finger, backed by the middle and index.

RIGHT PLACE, WRONG TIME
Otis Rush

Otis Rush was the first of the three West Side blues legends to record. With all due respect to Magic Sam and Buddy Guy, Rush is, at least marginally, the most soulful and subtle guitarist of the three, with a devastating vibrato. Due to various reasons, including his occasional reluctance to compose new material, his recording career has unfortunate gaps. "Right Place, Wrong Time" is the title track from one of his best, but least known albums, capturing him at his peak in 1971. It was not released until 1976, however, due to questionable decisions beyond his control. His influence on Eric Clapton and Stevie Ray Vaughan, among many other illustrious followers, is inestimable. Vaughan named his backing band Double Trouble after one of Rush's most famous songs.

TONE
Perhaps influenced by Ike Turner, Rush recorded his classic Cobra Records songs in 1956 with a sunburst Strat, and over the years, he has mostly gone back and forth between the ubiquitous Fender flagship guitar and a Gibson ES-345. But there was a period from the late sixties into the seventies when he shouldered a 1964–69 semi-hollow Epiphone Riviera with the mini-humbuckers that would later appear on the Les Paul Deluxe. Playing on both pickups, Rush is likely plugged into a Fender combo amp, as supplied by the recording studio, at moderate volume.

A Gibson ES-335, Guild Starfire, or even a reissue Epiphone Riviera through a 50-watt tube combo will approximate the sought-after tone. Basically, set the amp controls flat with just a touch of gain if the amp features a master volume, and adjust the volume pots on the guitar as needed.

TECHNIQUE
Playing upside down and backwards on a right-handed guitar with bare fingers like Albert King has contributed to the reverence guitarists have for his sinuous bending, slinky vibrato, and impassioned vocal phrasing. To perform the horn part in the intro with one guitar, play the octaves on strings 6 and 4 and 5 and 3 with the index and ring fingers, low to high; for the octaves on strings 4 and 2, utilize the ring and pinky fingers.

Rush does much of his good work soloing in the "Albert King box," or upper extension of the A minor pentatonic scale, with the addition of the major-key-defining major 3rd (C♯). He develops considerable torque by pulling *down* on string 1 with his ring finger, backed by the middle and index. Of course, for us conventionally fretting pickers, pushing *up* is the answer. But we, too, should always back up bending fingers for maximum strength, control, and accuracy.

In measures 6–8 of verse 3, Rhy. Fill 1 is played by rhythm guitarist Fred Burton, not Rush. Nonetheless, it is a dandy and should be learned and stored for future use when moving from the IV chord (measure 6) to the I chord (measures 7–8) in any 12-bar major-key blues. In measure 6, access the D9 chord in the usual way: with the middle, index, and a ring-finger barre, low to high. Next, barre strings 4–3 at fret 5 with the index finger and hammer the A note on fret 7 with the ring finger. In measure 7, play the A9 chord, low to high, with the index, ring, middle, and pinky fingers. Execute the gliss that crosses the bar line of measures 7–8 with the index finger.

SATISFY SUSIE
Lonnie Mack

It is a great injustice that Lonnie Mack is not in the Rock and Roll Hall of Fame. Acknowledged as the first blues-rock guitar hero with his hit instrumental version of Chuck Berry's "Memphis" in 1963, he was scorching his strings and backing

James Brown and Freddie King while his British counterparts were still learning from records. Following a long fallow period directly instigated by the British Invasion, he had a second act, thanks, in part, to Stevie Ray Vaughan, resulting in a contract with Alligator Records. The first album on the Chicago blues label, *Strike Like Lightning* (1986), features both mentor and prize protégé duking it out, including on the heart-pounding "Satisfy Susie."

TONE
Along with Albert King, Mack is the most prominent guitarist known for flaunting an original Gibson Flying V. He acquired his #007 in 1958, when he was 16, and had his local music store install a Bigsby vibrato. Due to his extensive use of the unit on his 1963 album, *The Wham of That Memphis Man*, it became known as the "whammy bar" among guitarists. Mack played the V through a vintage, tube Magnatone 280 amp containing a true vibrato circuit for a unique sound inspired by Robert Ward of the Ohio Untouchables. In later years, Mack would use a Roland Jazz Chorus 120 to achieve a facsimile of his signature swirling effect. In lieu of the JC, a Boss VB-2, Diamond Vibrato, or Fulltone Deja2 stompbox will work well. To get his whip-like vibrato, however, the whammy bar is a real necessity, making any solidbody Gibson, PRS, or similar guitar with 'buckers and a bar a consideration. Play on the bridge pickup, with the guitar volume cranked and the amp in "disturbing the neighbors" range.

TECHNIQUE
(*See editor's note about capoing at fret 1 in standard tuning to play along in the recorded key of F.*)
In the guitar solo, Mack (Gtr. 1) flashes a few of his classic moves based around fast, repetitive patterns. Measures 1–3 contain his patented "Albert King box" riff, begun by quickly bending the A to B with the ring finger, backed by the middle and index, releasing the bend, playing the G with the index, followed by the E on string 2 with the ring finger and string 2 open. Except for the release back to A, all notes are picked and the entire riff must be attacked with ferocity.

Measures 8–9 show his cool use of the open first string in a stinging fashion. In measure 8, use an upstroke on string 1 (open) and gliss from D to E on string 2 with the ring finger. In measure 9, again, hit string 1 (open) with an upstroke and gliss from A to B on string 3 with the index finger.

A turbo-charged version of a similar riff, popularized by Chuck Berry through Charlie Christian, flies off Mack's fingers in measures 13–16. Pick down and bend the D to E with the pinky, backed by the ring, middle, and index. Though it may seem counterintuitive to pick upward for the E on string 1, it has the advantage of bringing the hand back into position to start anew on string 4, while also injecting a subtle degree of swing.

Saving his "heavy artillery" for the high point of his solo, Mack remains in the root-octave position of the E minor pentatonic scale and alternates gritty dyads with the open first string. Employ the index as a small barre for both sets of strings and try picking the dyads with a downstroke and string 1 with an upstroke.

SHELTER ME
Tab Benoit
Tab Benoit once told this author that if he was a guitar teacher, he would not allow his beginning students to touch the neck with their fretting hand for six months, but to just work on strumming with the right hand, as he believes the guitar to be like a "drum," first and foremost. The underappreciated Baton Rouge native, who is an expert drummer, learned his blues the old-fashioned way: at the feet of Louisiana legends Tabby Thomas, Raful Neal, and Henry Gray. *Power of the Pontchartrain* finds the top Cajun trio guitarist backed by the funky "gumbo" served up by the Louisiana group LeRoux, though his skills shine most brightly on "Shelter Me," essentially a trio tune with minimal overdubbing in the choruses.

TONE
As iconoclastic in his choice of axes as in his highly rhythmic, swampy blues, Benoit has favored 1972 semi-hollow Fender Tele Deluxe thinline guitars featuring two humbucking pickups, strung with a custom set of .011s, including a heftier low E. By 2007, he was using two custom-built, signature Category 5 combo amps: a Voice of the Wetlands 45 with four 10-inch speakers and a Voice of the Wetlands 90 with two 12-inch speakers, built to sound like a blackface Super Reverb and Twin Reverb, respectively. He plays on the neck pickup throughout the song, with the amps adjusted for moderate overdrive.

TECHNIQUE
Similar to Rory Gallagher's "Laundromat," Benoit incorporates the open fifth string in harmony with a fretted note on string 4, as seen in measures 2–3 of the intro, throughout verse 1, and in measures 1, 3, 12–14 of the first guitar solo. Use the ring finger for the A notes at fret 7 of string 4 while simultaneously strumming string 5.

Measures 1–4 of the second guitar solo contain a tangy, repetitive double-stop pattern that creates a memorable entrance with taut musical tension. Play the G/E dyad with the middle and index fingers, low to high, and hammer to the A with the ring finger. In measure 15, barre strings 2–1 with the index finger and hold the bend on string 3 with the ring finger, backed by the middle, so it rings out beseechingly.

STILL RAININ'

Jonny Lang

Jonny Lang was the torch bearer for the spate of young kids who materialized in the '90s with startling blues chops and authentic expression far beyond their years. He was all of 16 years old in 1997, when *Lie to Me* revealed him to have a voice like Otis Redding and serious guitar-slinger technique. A year later, *Wander This World*, featuring the heavy blues-rocking "Still Rainin'," confirmed the hype was real. Conversion to Christianity in 2000 resulted in his music embracing religious themes. *Fight for My Soul* (2013), his first new release in seven years, contains his turn towards classic-sounding, original R&B and soul music.

TONE

Lang began playing a Strat in the beginning of his pro career, but hearing Albert Collins and Tab Benoit led him to a Tele—specifically, a 1972 Deluxe thinline with humbuckers. He quickly advanced to a custom Benedict Tele Deluxe copy with a Gibson P-90 inserted between the two 'buckers, followed by a Fender Custom Shop version with similar specs, heard on "Still Rainin'." Live, he was using a Fender Vibro-King amp.

In place of the investment required for a Jonny Lang Custom Shop Tele Deluxe and a 60-watt, 3x10 Vibro-King, play any vintage Tele Deluxe floored on the double-coil bridge pickup through a vintage or reissue blackface Fender Deluxe Reverb. Set the treble at 7, middle at 4, bass at 4, and reverb at 4, with the level on an Ibanez Tube Screamer cranked and drive adjusted appropriately to replicate the desired crunch.

TECHNIQUE

Be aware that Lang executes his signature, vigorous vibrato with his ring finger (backed by the middle) by removing his thumb from from the edge of the fingerboard and shaking his whole hand from the elbow, perpendicular to the neck à la Stevie Ray Vaughan, as first encountered in measures 5–6 of the intro.

In the intro, Rhy. Fig. 1 (Gtr. 1) is classic power-chord hard rock. In order to have the left hand in an advantageous position for the hip fill in measure 7, and to just plain *look* cool, use the thumb to play the bass notes on the F, A♭, and B♭ chords. Access the notes on strings 5–4 with the ring and pinky fingers, respectively. For the fill, hammer from B♭ to C♭ (B natural) with the index and middle fingers, utilizing the pinky for the A♭ and the ring finger for the F.

In measure 7 of the guitar solo, Lang (Gtr. 3) climaxes his short but searing improvisation with a fat triple stop that roars. Bend the B♭ at fret 15 with the ring finger, backed by the middle and index, and allow it to sustain. Barre the A♭/E♭ notes at fret 16 with the pinky.

In measures 5–7 of the interlude, Lang (Gtr. 2) takes a page from the Jimi Hendrix playbook for a rich dollop of harmony. Barre at fret 10 with the index finger for the F major triad and at fret 8 for the E♭ major triad, hammering onto the 3rds at frets 12 and 10, respectively.

STROLLIN' WITH BONES

T-Bone Walker

He was neither the first to play electric guitar nor even the first to play electric blues guitar, but Aaron "T-Bone" Walker was the first to grasp the potential of amplified strings for expressing the emotional power of the blues. In the process, he created many enduring classics well beyond his signature composition, "(Call It) Stormy Monday" (1947). Later in the same watershed year, he recorded the landmark swinging shuffle "Strollin' with Bone" (note the original spelling). As the inarguable "Father of Electric Blues," his importance cannot be exaggerated. He died of pneumonia in 1976 at the age of 64.

TONE

As befitted his suave, sophisticated demeanor and music, Walker favored the classier Gibson ES-250 with one non-adjustable bar pickup early on, as opposed to the ES-150 popularized by his electric jazz guitar counterpart, Charlie Christian. Photos from the period show him with a first-generation 1939 model, which he appears to flaunt until the early fifties, when he is seen with a Gibson ES-5 equipped with a trio of P-90 pickups. Walker likely played through a matching 20-watt Gibson EH-185 amp with one 12-inch speaker.

A hollow acoustic-electric such as the thin ES-330 or Epiphone Casino, or a deeper-body ES-125, ES-225, or ES-175 with P-90 pickups, is recommended to approach Walker's warm, woody tone with an edge. A moderately-powered Fender tweed or similar-sounding amp will deliver the goods if played at a moderate volume with flat-tone EQ, though the ever-versatile blackface Fender Deluxe Reverb will also suffice in a pinch.

TECHNIQUE

Note from photos and videos how Walker held his guitar out from his body in an unusual position, parallel to the floor, and swept across the strings with his right hand in an outward motion. Since this technique required him to bend his left wrist at a severe angle, inviting carpal tunnel syndrome, it is to be discouraged.

Far and away the greatest lesson to derive from "Strollin' with Bones" is the tremendous sense of swing and peerless phrasing involving dynamic rests. In addition, it features a number of choice T-Bone licks that have—and should continue to have—wide application. In measures 5–7 of rehearsal letter E, note the repetitive, tension-inducing four-note pattern in the root position of the Bb blue scale, where the Db note at fret 9 should be bent a quarter step (to the "true blue note") with the pinky. Barre the subsequent Bb and F notes at fret 6 of strings 2–1 with the index finger, picking down-up-up.

Measures 5–9 of rehearsal letter F contain the classic T-Bone lick, most famously appropriated by Chuck Berry: the syncopated unison bend on the 5th of the I chord. Anchor the index finger on the second-string F, bending the third-string Eb one whole step with the ring finger, backed by the middle finger.

Another classic repetitive blues lick is found in measures 6–7 of rehearsal letter H, where strings 2–1 are barred at fret 6 by the index finger, and string 3 is bent a half step at fret 8 with the ring finger, backed by the middle finger. Pick, from low to high, down-down-up.

Scintillating dissonant blues harmony occurs in measures 5–7 of rehearsal letter I: the half-step bend of two of the three notes of the implied Bbdim7 chord. Utilize the following fingers, from low to high: middle, index, and ring. Maintain pressure on the Db note on string 1 while simultaneously bending the E and G notes on strings 3–2 with the middle and index fingers, respectively.

SWEET SIXTEEN
B.B. King

The "King of the Blues" is a designation he modestly rejects, taking it more as a play on his last name than fact. Nonetheless, Riley "B.B." King is, hands down, the most influential postwar electric blues guitarist ever, with his sensuous bends and vibrato creeping into the technique of rock, jazz, and country guitar players. Originally recorded in 1960 as a two-sided single, this epic version of "Sweet Sixteen" was recorded for *L.A. Midnight* in 1972 and also appears on the 1983 compilation *Why I Sing the Blues*. A few years into his crossover success, the song shows the King easily retaining his crown, as he stretches out with a devastating performance that is second to none. Now 88 years old, he shows no sign of slowing down.

TONE

Though there have been many "Lucilles" since the late forties, the Gibson ES-355 has come to be regarded as the iconic "lady" and true love of his life. A 1966-67 ES-355 TD/SV (thin, double pickup/stereo, varitone) model through a blackface Fender Twin was all King needed to create the sweet, singing sound for which he is renowned. Typically, he adjusted his guitar with both humbuckers selected and the varitone on its lowest setting, with both tone controls wide open and the volume pots at 5–6 so he could blend their tones to taste. The Twin was likely set as follows: volume at 4, treble at 6, middle at 4, bass at 4, and reverb at 4.

King has commented (complained?) in print that producers in the past would not allow him to play as loud as he wished in the studio. Hence, while he presents a warm, rich tone, it does not compare to *Live at the Regal*, where he pushes his Twin into ecstatic distortion. A semi-hollowbody axe with both humbuckers "open," straight into a Fender tube combo, will produce the refined yet expressive tone.

TECHNIQUE

Get ready for a post-grad course in electric blues guitar. Some of the required curriculum: Measures 1–2 of the intro feature *the* classic King intro licks derived from the composite blues scale (blues scale plus Mixolydian mode). Employ the index and ring fingers sequentially, bending the D♯ note at fret 11 with the ring finger, backed by the middle and index fingers.

The end of measure 7 through the beginning of measure 8 feature one of his signature moves in his "B.B. King box"; here, performed around fret 14. Play the C♯ note at fret 14 with the index finger, then bend the G♯ note at fret 16 with the ring finger, backed by the middle finger. In measure 8, release the bend back to G♯ and quickly shift the ring finger to the D♯ note on string 2, bending one whole step and applying vigorous vibrato with a short sweep.

King modestly claims not to be able to play rhythm guitar, but it is just not true. Check out the end of measure 12 of the second verse and beat 1 of measure 1 of the third verse, where he bangs a slick F♯7 voicing consisting of the notes C♯, A♯, and E (index, middle, and ring finger, low to high) and a first-inversion C♯ major triad comprised of the notes C♯, G♯, and E♯ (F), fingered, low to high, with the middle finger and a small index-finger barre.

Another classic King lick in his "B.B. King box" in the guitar solo goes from the end of measure 4 through the beginning of measure 5. Plant the index finger on the C# note at fret 14, bend the G# at fret 16 one-and-a-half steps with the ring finger, pick the G# and follow down through the composite blues scale with the index (F#), pinky (E), index (C#), middle (A#), and index (C#). Vibrato the C# with the index finger by removing the thumb from the back of the neck and twisting the wrist back and forth, the thumb waving in the air like the flutter of a "hummingbird."

At the end of measure 7 of the guitar solo, King lets fly one of his classic root-octave glisses, sliding from the C# at fret 21 with his pinky as poignant punctuation and proof positive that sometimes less is more.

TEXAS FLOOD
Stevie Ray Vaughan

Stevie Ray Vaughan roared out of Texas in the early eighties like a tornado, and along with Robert Cray, kicked off a second blues revival. Possessing intimidating chops and the deepest feeling for the blues, he brought the influence of Albert King, Buddy Guy, Lonnie Mack, and Jimi Hendrix, among others, to bear on a style that has been widely imitated but never duplicated. The classic Larry Davis slow blues "Texas Flood" was deemed evocative and appropriate for the title track of his epochal, double-platinum debut from 1983. Following three more releases with his rhythm section, Double Trouble, and a serious bout of substance abuse from which he recovered, Vaughan died tragically in a senseless helicopter crash in 1990. The title of his posthumous 1991 album speaks for us all: *The Sky is Crying*.

TONE

Vaughan called his "Number One" Strat a '59, though only the pickups were that vintage, with the neck a 1962 re-fretted with jumbos (Dunlop 6100), and the body a 1963. He strung it with exceptionally heavy gauges for an electric guitar player: .013, .015, .019, .028w, .038w, and .058w, though he lessened the tension by tuning down a half step. Although he is famous for playing through two late-1963 Fender blackface, black Tolex Vibroverbs with 15-inch JBL 130-E speakers, he also played a 1980 100-watt Marshall 4140 Club & Country combo with two 12-inch speakers for a clean sound (the Fenders were for distortion). He also availed himself to Jackson Brown's 150-watt Dumbleland head with 6550 tubes for his clean sound while recording the album in his studio. The one pedal that he used for an extra kick was an Ibanez TS-9 Tube Screamer (not an 808, as widely believed), with Drive, Tone, and Level set at mid-point.

A good Strat with the selector switch set to the "out-of-phase" position (i.e., between the middle and bridge pickups) is *de rigueur* to start the signal chain through a 40-watt or larger Fender or Marshall combo with at least two 12-inch speakers, with volume at 6 (or above!), treble at 4.5, middle at 4, bass at 3, and reverb at 2.5. Be aware that the heft of Vaughan's big, robust, "open" sound came from the high volume produced by the output tubes, as opposed to the variously compressed sound one would get from pushing the preamp section at a lower output volume, or from an overreliance on distortion stompboxes.

TECHNIQUE

As likely one of the first Vaughan songs many fans heard, "Texas Flood" shows the future guitar hero at his most traditional and "restrained." Measures 8–9 of the intro offer a prime example of his Albert King influence, as he appears quite comfortable in the "Albert King box," or extension position of the G blues scale, bending in sequential half-steps up string 1 with his ring finger, backed by the middle and index. In measure 9, he resolves in classic King fashion to the G note on string 2 with the ring finger.

In measure 1 of the first verse, over the I chord, he comps a cool G7 voicing, played with the middle, ring, and index fingers, low to high, to add welcome harmony to the onslaught of single-note lines. Logically, he follows in measure 3, over the IV chord, with an implied C9 voicing favored by his big mentor and accessed with a small index-finger barre. Again, though rightfully lauded for his overwhelming fast and furious scale work, as an extraordinary trio guitarist, he knew how to flesh out his music with juicy chordal indicators.

Measures 5–6 of the second verse (the IV chord) contain a musically intelligent and artistically expressive series of chords, triple stops, and dyads related to the C dominant tonality. Nail the C9 voicing with the typical fingering: middle, index, and small ring-finger barre. Quickly switch to the small index-finger barre for the implied C9 triple stop in order to play the E/C dyad with the ring finger, the D/Bb dyad with the index finger, the G note on string 4 with the ring finger, and finishing up in measure 6 with the index finger for the D/Bb dyad.

In measure 11 of the guitar solo (the turnaround), Vaughan unleashes his enviable, athletic vibrato. Videos show him removing the palm of his hand from the back of the neck and literally moving his whole hand up and down from his elbow, with his ring, middle, and index fingers locked in place on string 2.

The second measure of free time at the end of the tune contains a most useful T-Bone Walker G9 voicing. Theoretically, G9/B is a first-inversion dominant chord, played, low to high, with the index, ring, and middle fingers, with the pinky barring strings 1–2.

from Mike Bloomfield/Al Kooper/Stephen Stills - *Super Session*

Albert's Shuffle

Words and Music by Al Kooper and Mike Bloomfield

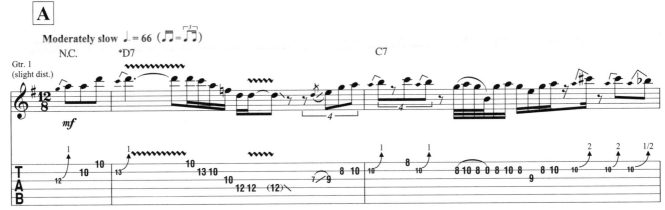

*Chord symbols reflect basic harmony.

**Played behind the beat.

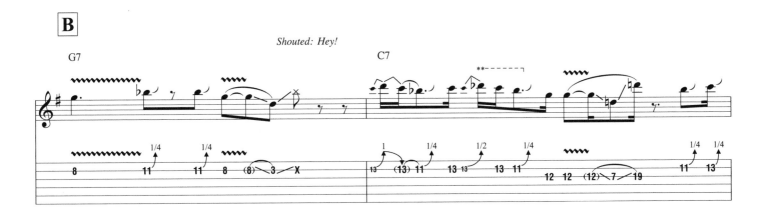

Shouted: Hey!

***Played ahead of the beat.

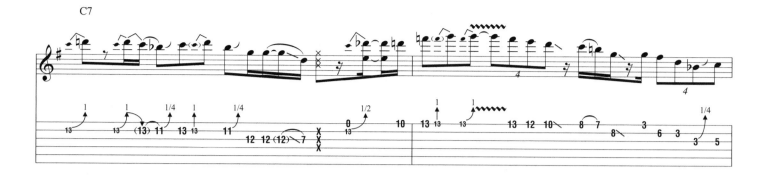

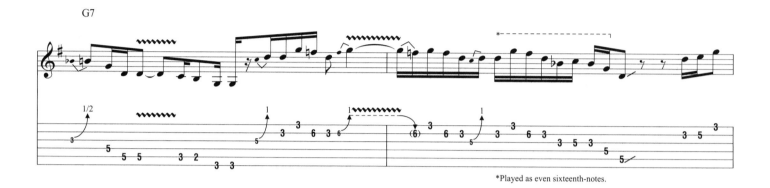

*Played as even sixteenth-notes.

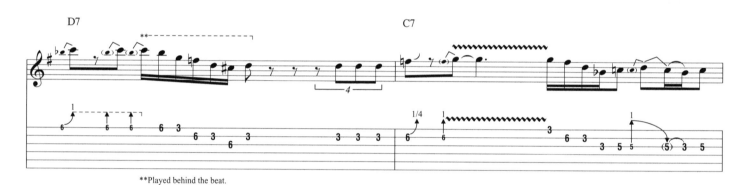

**Played behind the beat.

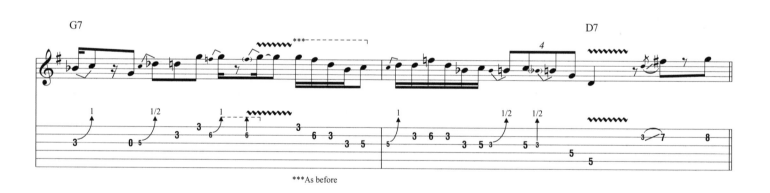

***As before

C

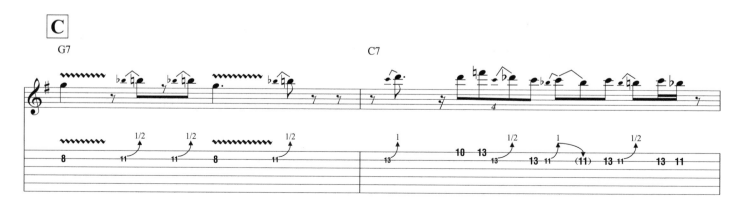

G7

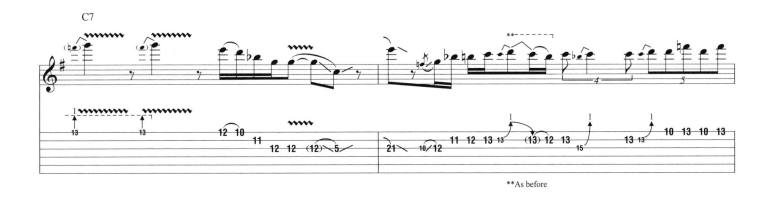

*Played ahead of the beat.

C7

**As before

G7

***Played behind the beat.

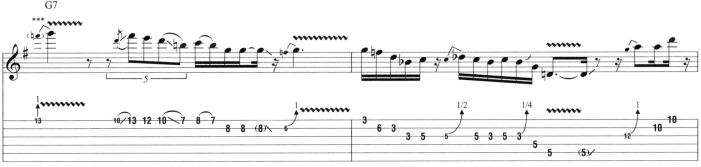

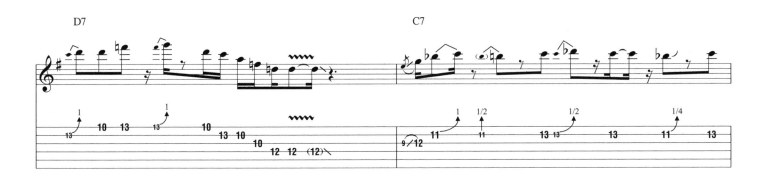

D7

C7

G7

D7

rake ---

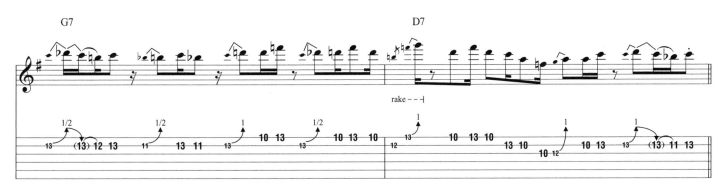

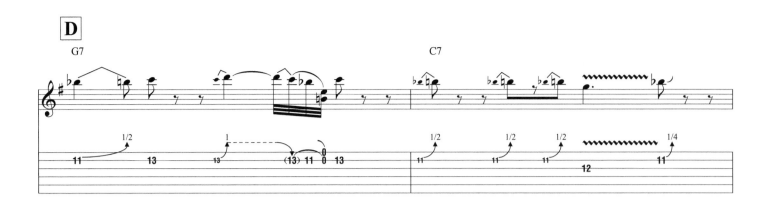

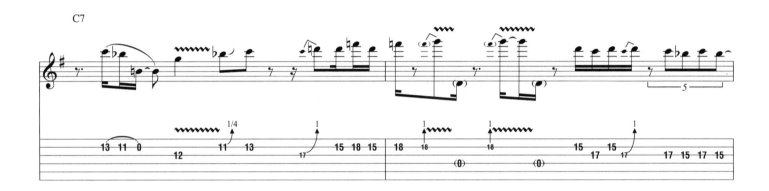

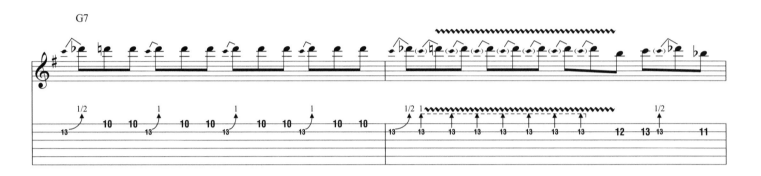

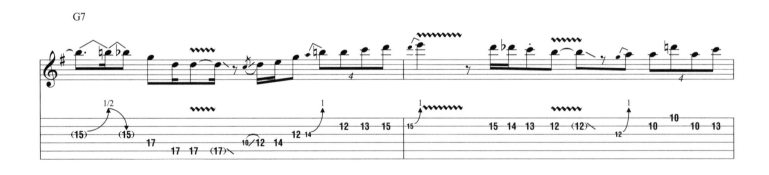

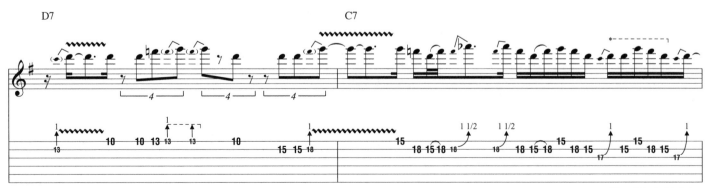

*Played ahead of the beat.

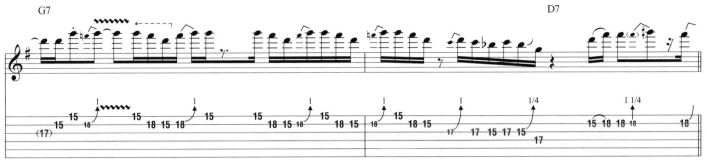

*Played ahead of the beat.

E

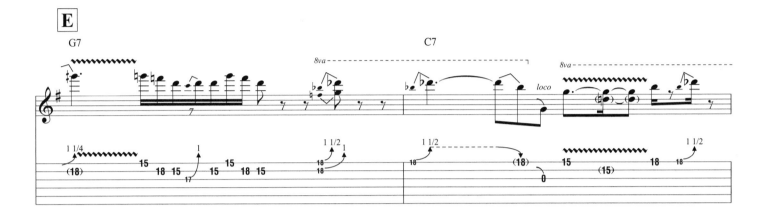

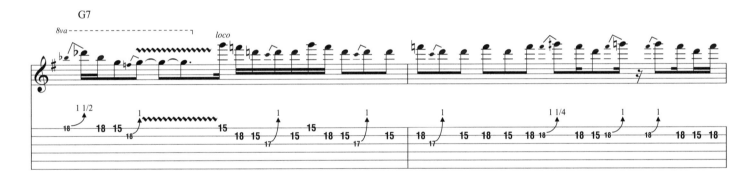

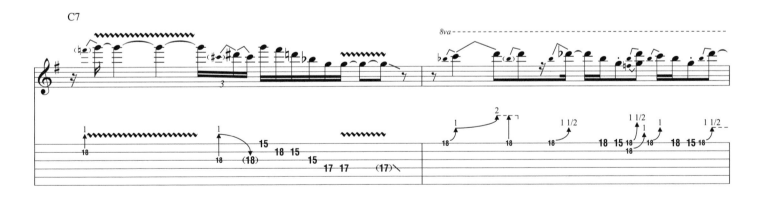

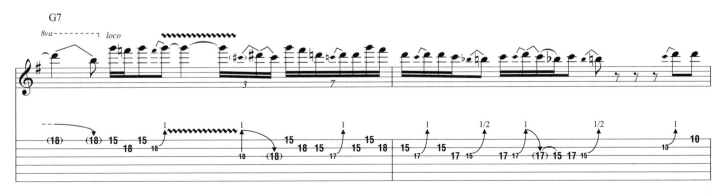

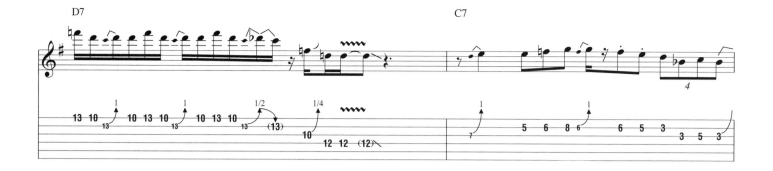

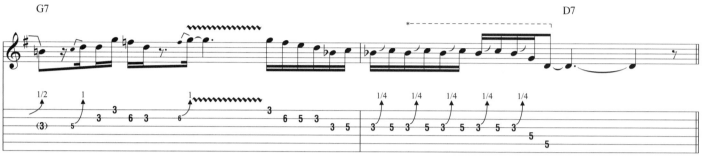

*Played behind the beat.

F

**T = Thumb on 6th string

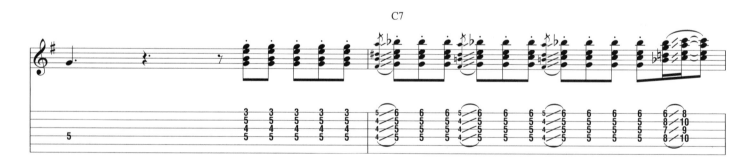

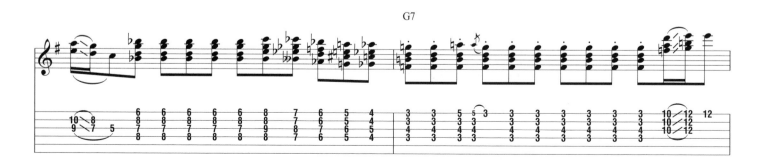

*let ring - - - - - - - ┤

*Refers to 6th string only.

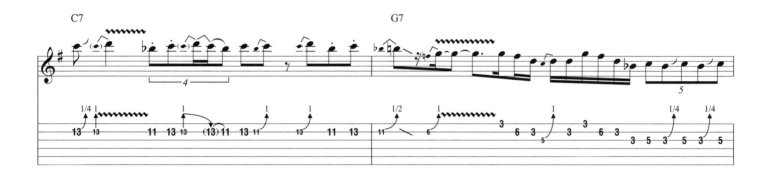

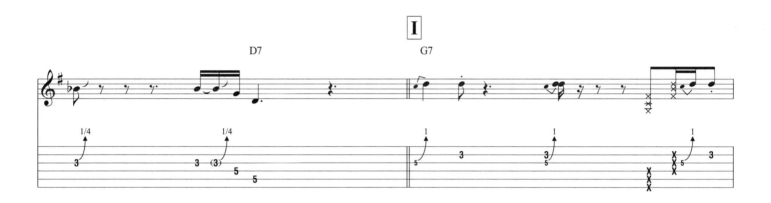

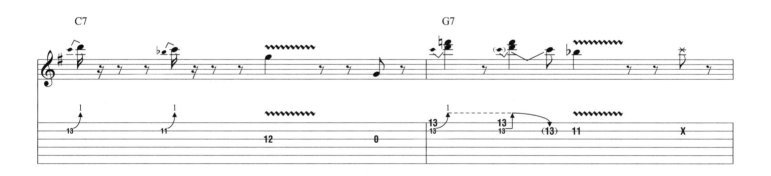

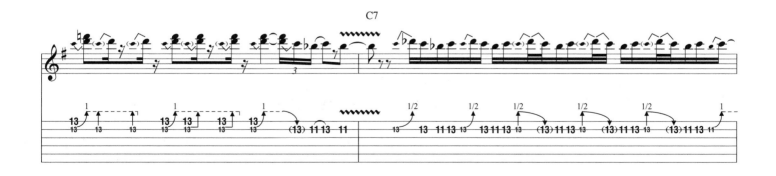

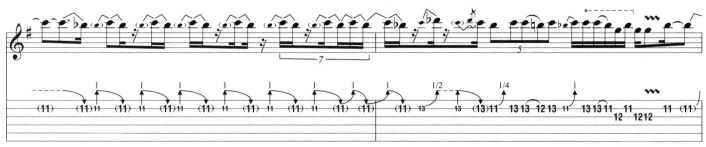

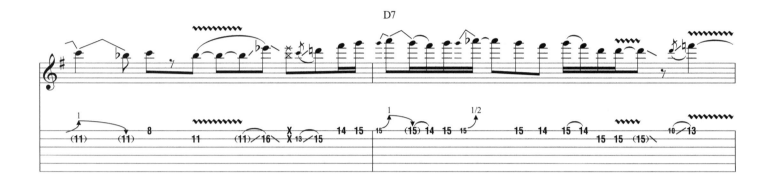

*Played behind the beat.

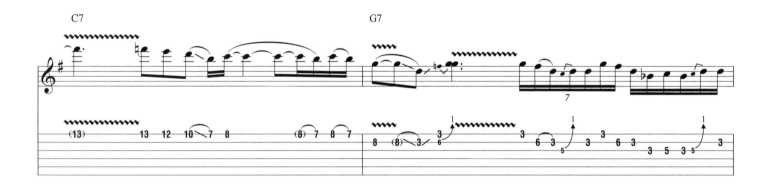

J

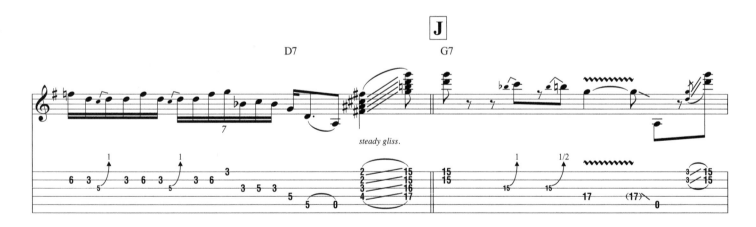

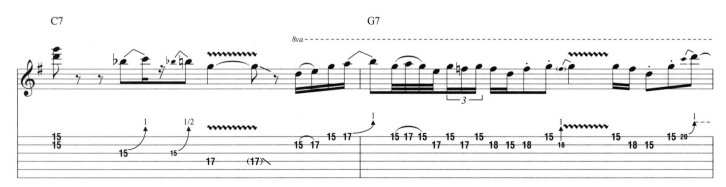

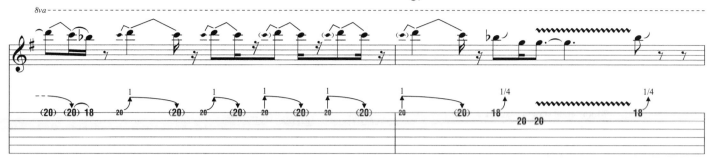

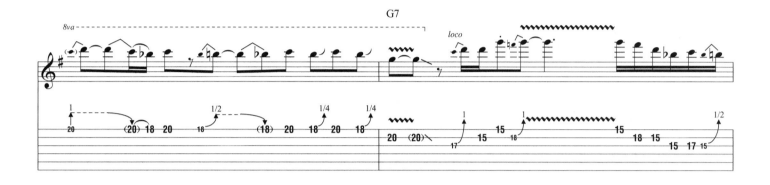

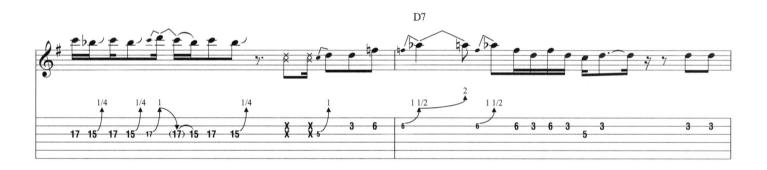

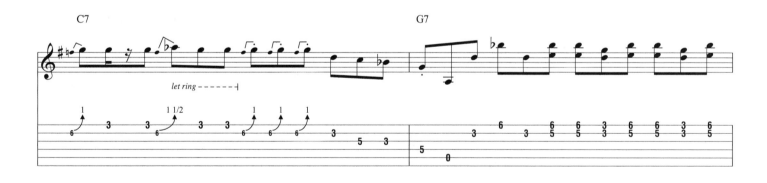

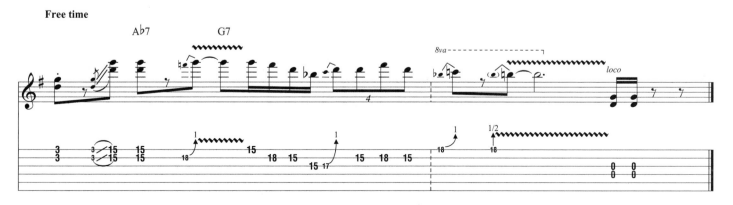

All of Your Love
(All Your Love)

Words and Music by Samuel Maghett

*Chord symbols reflect overall harmony.

Verse

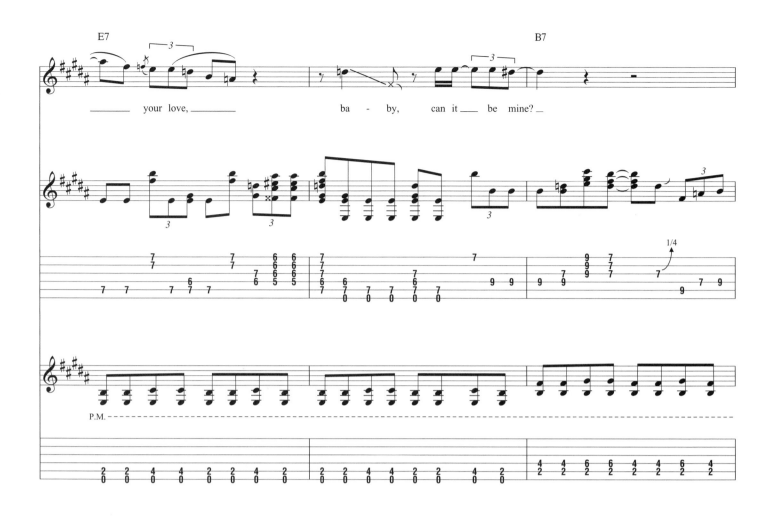

your love, _____ ba - by, can it _____ be mine? _____

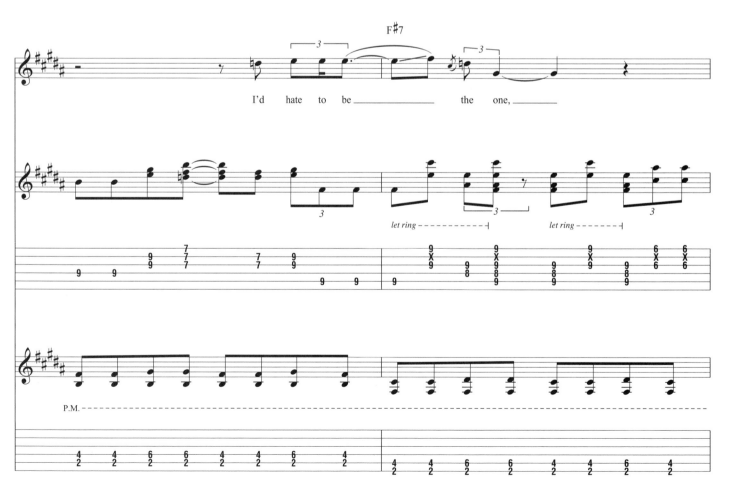

I'd hate to be _____ the one, _____

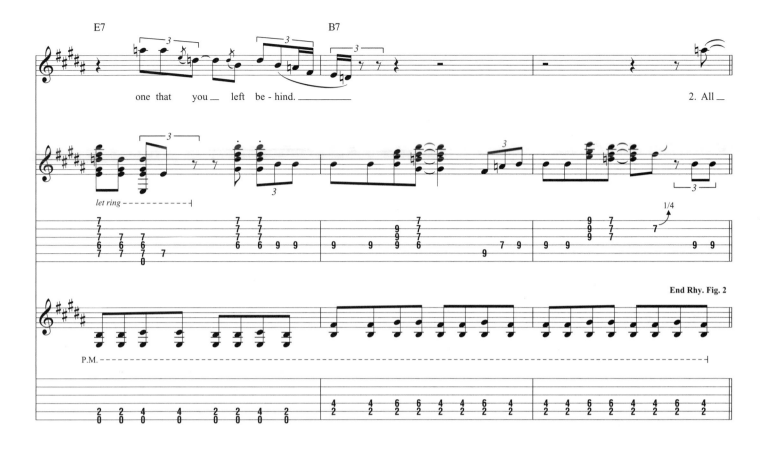

one that you ___ left be - hind. ___

2. All ___

Verse

Gtr. 2: w/ Rhy. Fig. 2

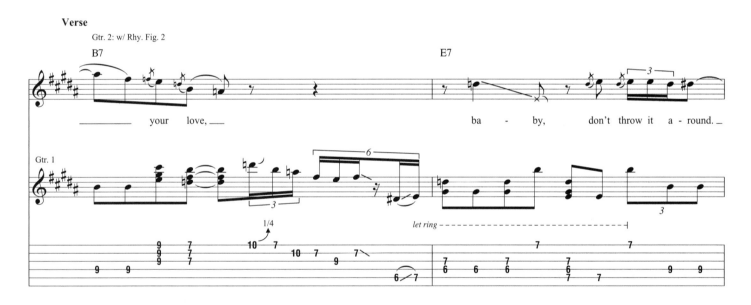

___ your love, ___

ba - by, don't throw it a - round. ___

Gtr. 1

___

All ___ your love, ___

ba - by, don't throw it a - round.

There's just one _____ thing, ba - by, _____

you may find _____ on the ground. _____

Guitar Solo
Gtr. 2: w/ Rhy. Fig. 1 (2 times)

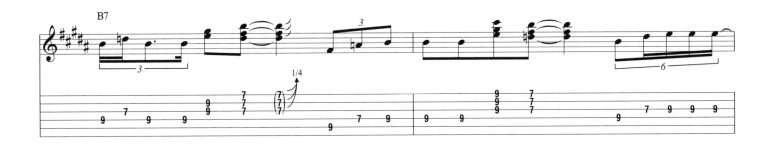

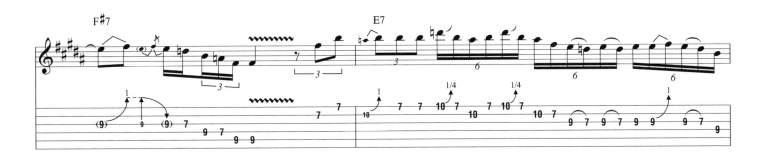

your love ___ I've got to have ___ one day. ___

___ Don't you leave ___ me, ba - by, ___

ba - by, please ___ come back this way. ___

Outro

Gtr. 2: w/ Rhy. Fig. 1 (till fade)

Repeat & fade

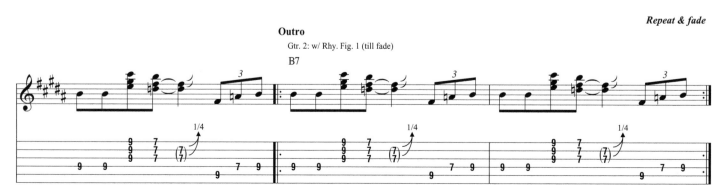

from Slim Harpo - *The Best of Slim Harpo*

Baby Scratch My Back

By James Moore

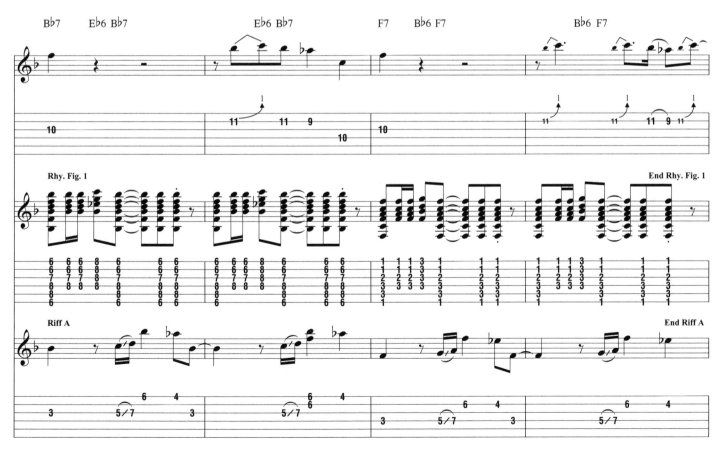

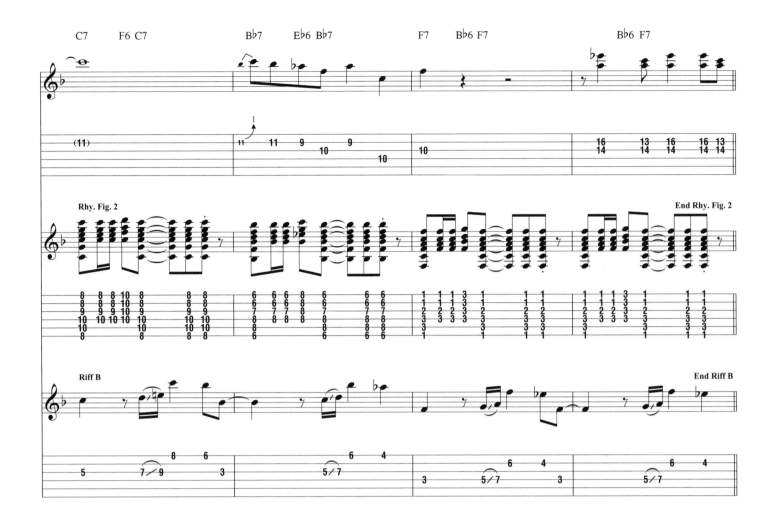

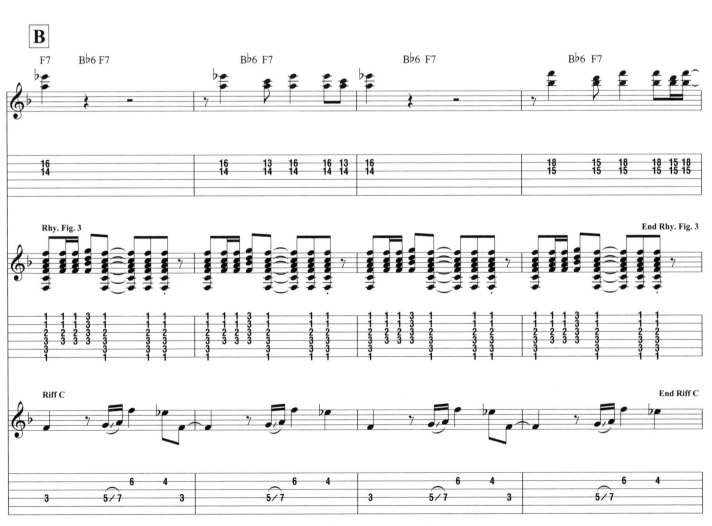

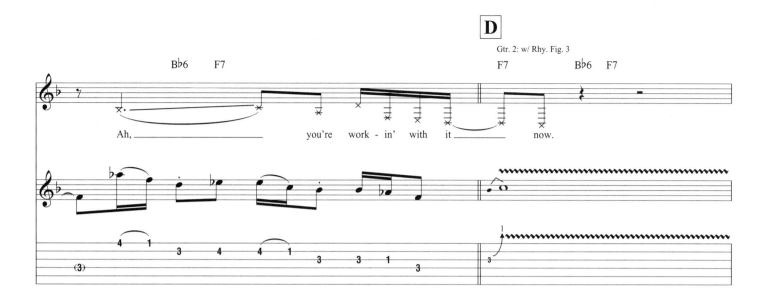

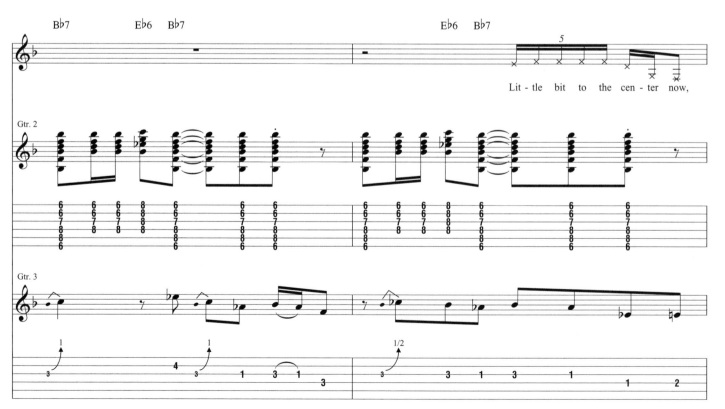

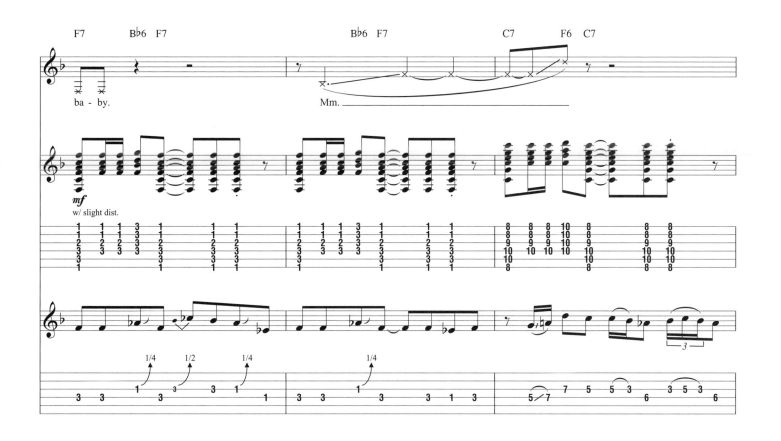

baby.

Mm. _____

*Gtr. 2: w/ Rhy. Fig. 2 (last 3 meas.)

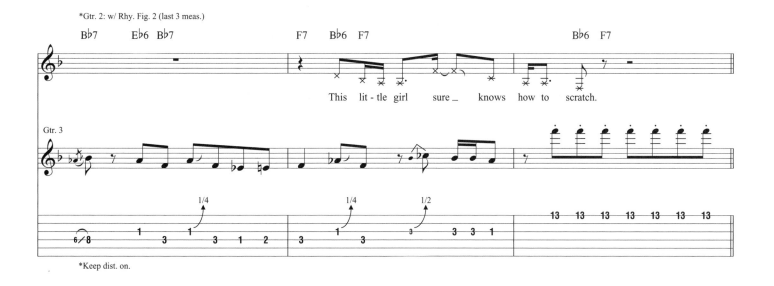

This lit-tle girl sure __ knows how to scratch.

Gtr. 3

*Keep dist. on.

E

Gtr. 2: w/ Rhy. Fig. 3

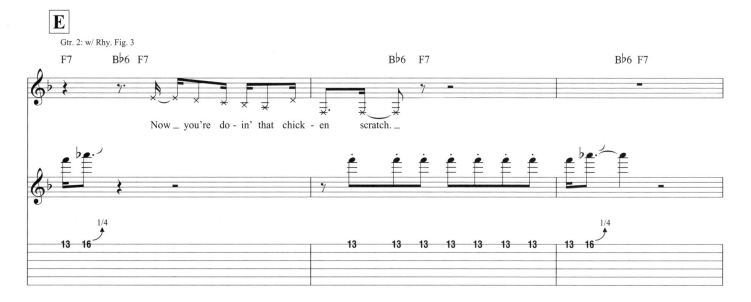

Now __ you're do-in' that chick-en scratch. __

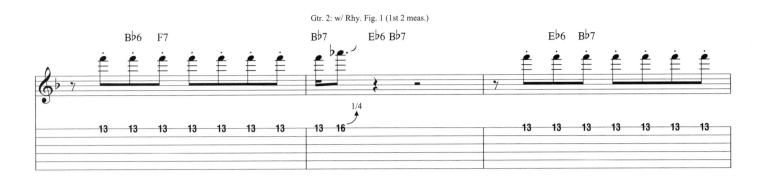

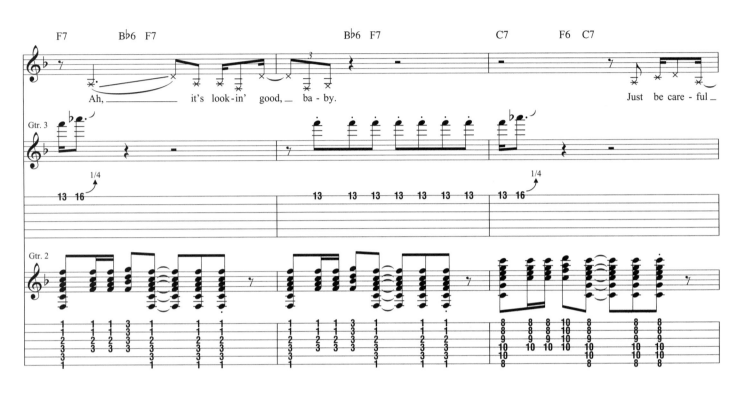

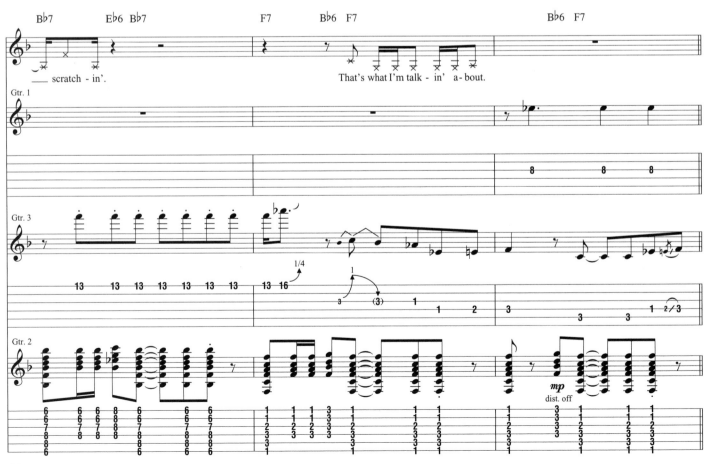

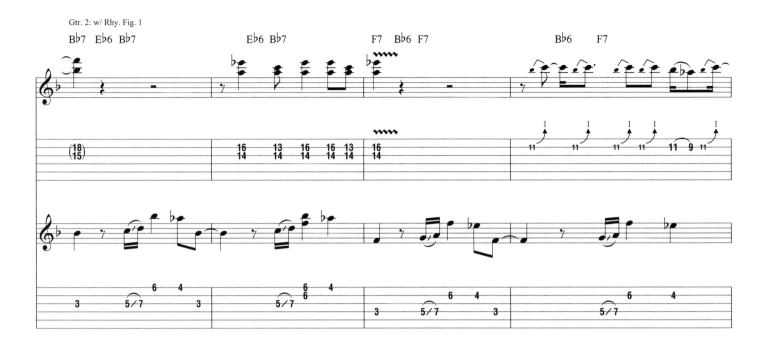

44

Bad to the Bone

Words and Music by George Thorogood

Open G tuning:
(low to high) D-G-D-G-B-D

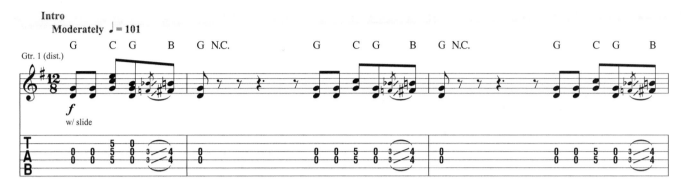

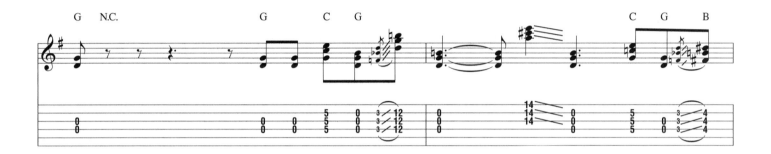

*Hypothetical fret locations.

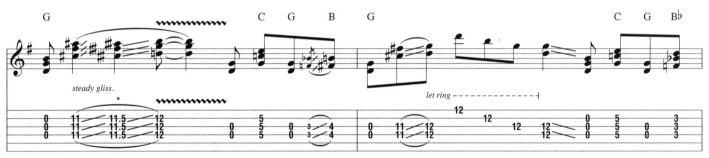

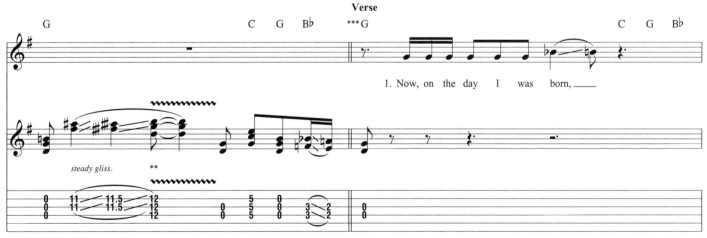

1. Now, on the day I was born, ____

**4th string rings due to vibrato; don't pick.   ***Chord symbols reflect overall harmony.

Gtr. 1 tacet

G   C   G   B♭   G   C   G   B♭

the nurs-es all gath-ered 'round, ___ and they gazed ___ in wide won - der

G   C   G   B♭   G   C   G   B♭

at the joy ___ they had found. ___ The head nurse spoke up,

G   C   G   B♭   G   C   G   B♭

said, "Leave ___ this one a - lone." ___ She could tell ___ right a - way ___

Chorus

G   C   G   B♭   G   C   G   B♭

that I was bad to the bone. Bad ___ to the bone. ___

Rhy. Fill 1   End Rhy. Fill 1   Rhy. Fig. 1

Gtr. 1

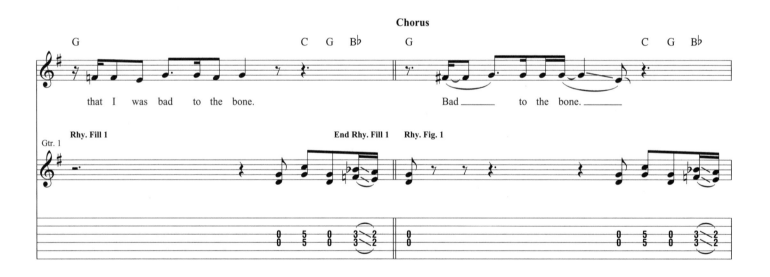

G   C   G   B♭   G   C   G   B♭

Bad ___ to the bone. ___ B, b, b, b, b, b, b, bad. ___

End Rhy. Fig. 1

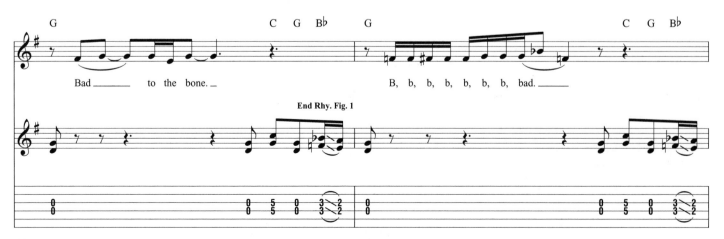

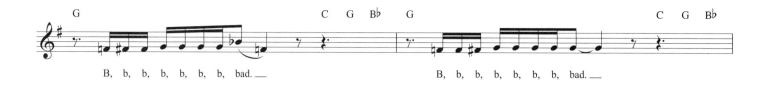

B, b, b, b, b, b, b, bad. ___

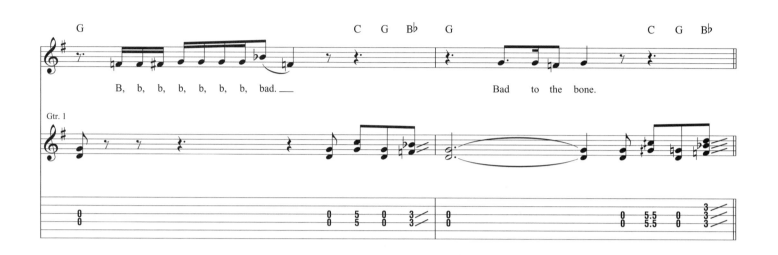

B, b, b, b, b, b, b, bad. ___   Bad   to   the   bone.

Gtr. 1

Guitar Solo

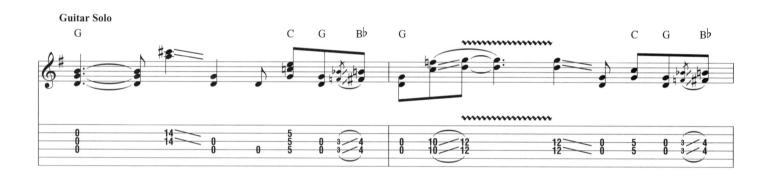

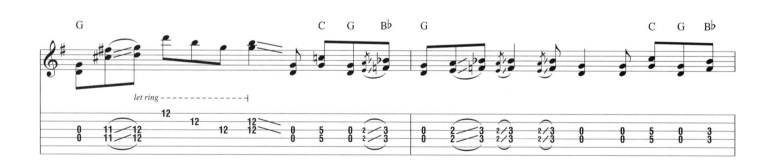

let ring - - - - - - - - - - - - - - - - - - |

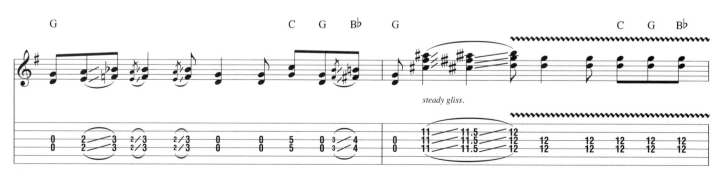

steady gliss.

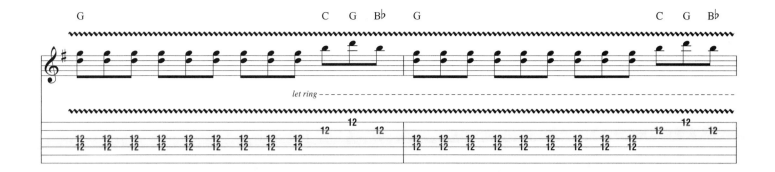

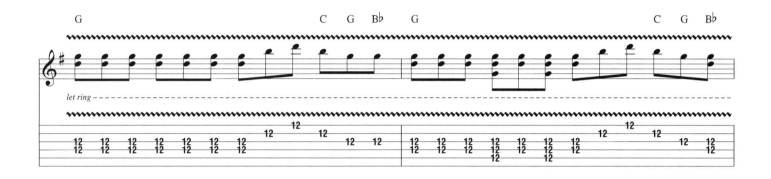

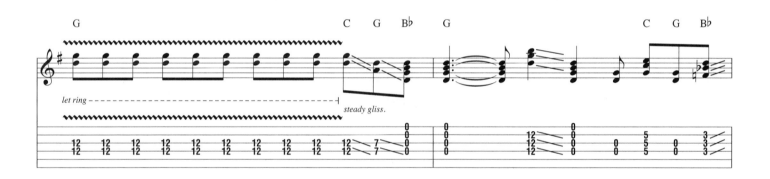

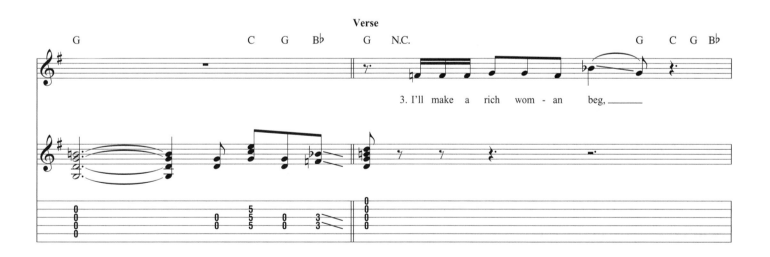

Verse

3. I'll make a rich wom-an beg, _____

and I'll make a good wom-an steal. __

I'll make an old __ wom-an blush, __

and I'll make a young girl squeal. _ I wan-na be yours, pret-ty ba-by,

Gtr. 1: w/ Rhy. Fill 1

yours and yours _ a - lone. _____ I'm here to tell ya, hon-ey, ____

Chorus

Gtr. 1: w/ Rhy. Fig. 1 (1st meas.)   Gtr. 1: w/ Rhy. Fig. 1 (1st meas.)

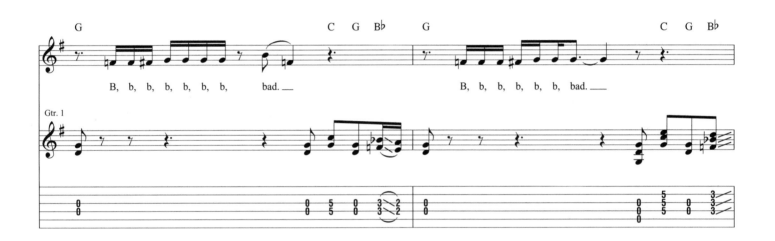

that I'm bad to the bone.   B, b, b, b, b, b, b, bad. _

B, b, b, b, b, b, b, bad. _   B, b, b, b, b, b, b, bad. _

Gtr. 1

Saxophone Solo

Bad to the bone.

Gtr. 1: w/ Rhy. Fig. 1 (2 times)

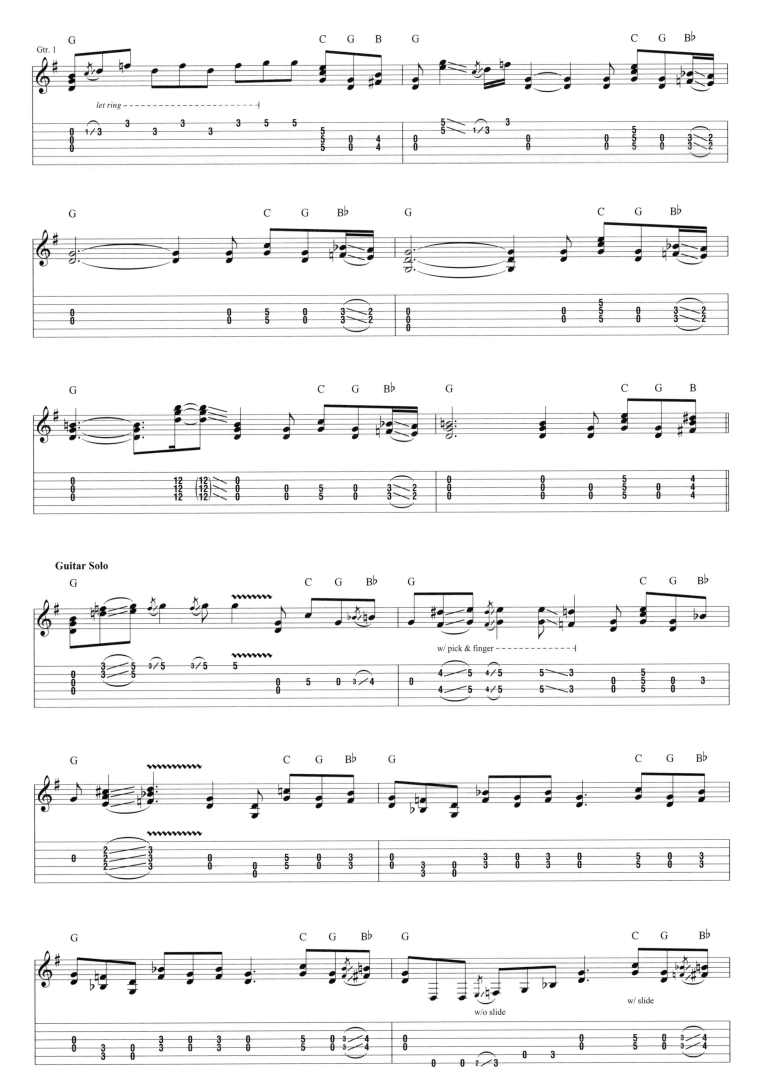

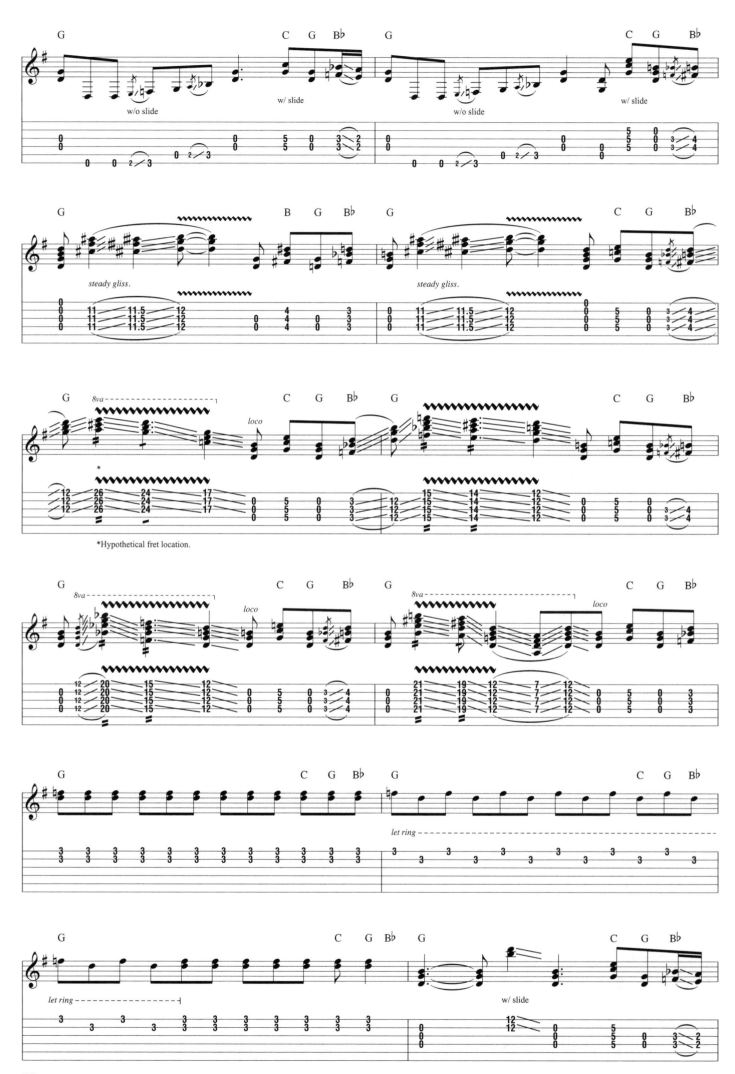

*Hypothetical fret location.

from Z.Z. Hill - *Down Home Blues*

Down Home Blues

Words and Music by George Jackson

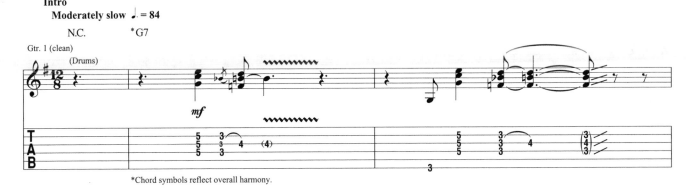

*Chord symbols reflect overall harmony.

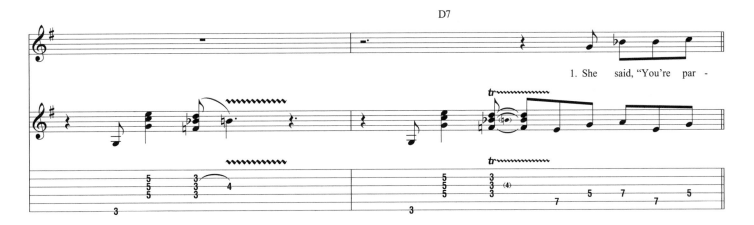

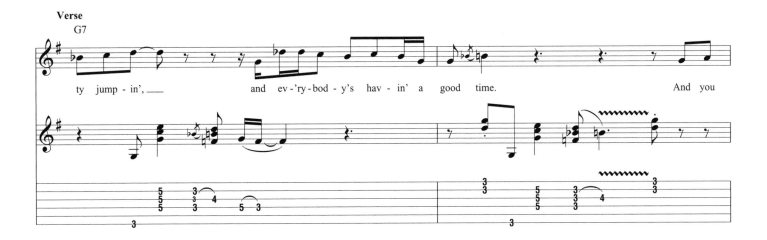

f'ta - ble _____ and kick off these shoes? _

While you're

fix - in' me a drink, _____ *Male & Female:* play me some of them down home __ blues." _

*Bkgd. vocal is Female.

_____ 2. She say, "You know I

56

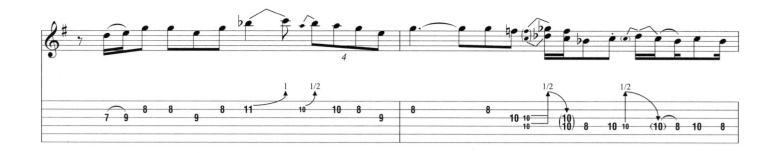

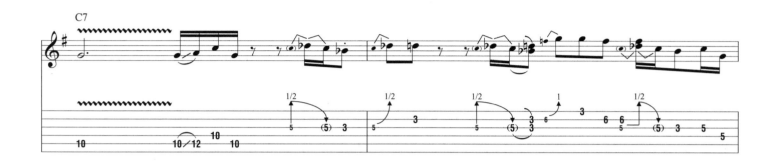

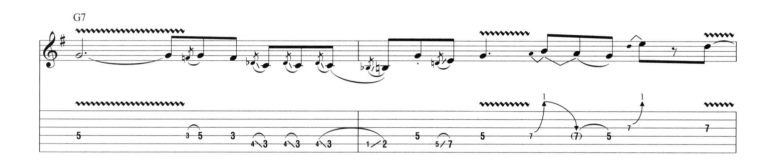

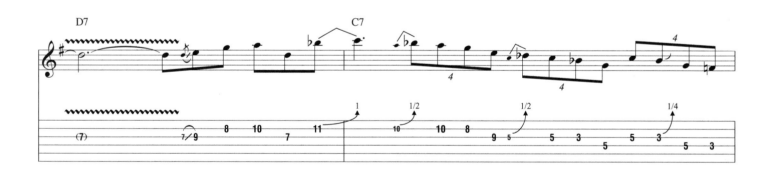

3. She said, "You know, my

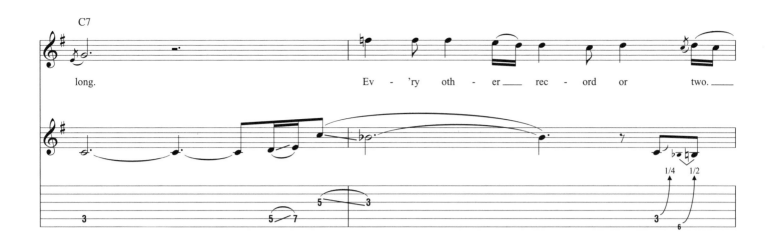

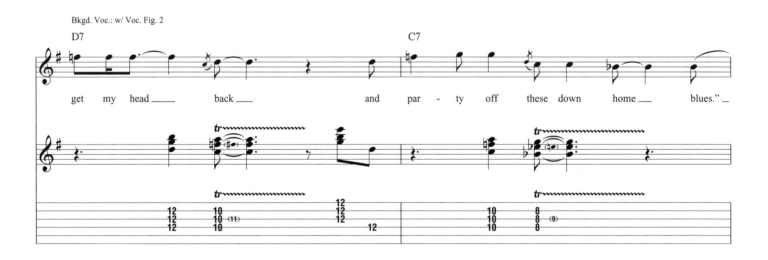

Bkgd. Voc.: w/ Voc. Fig. 2

Outro-Chorus

Bkgd. Voc.: w/ Voc. Fig. 1

blues. Down home blues.

Begin fade

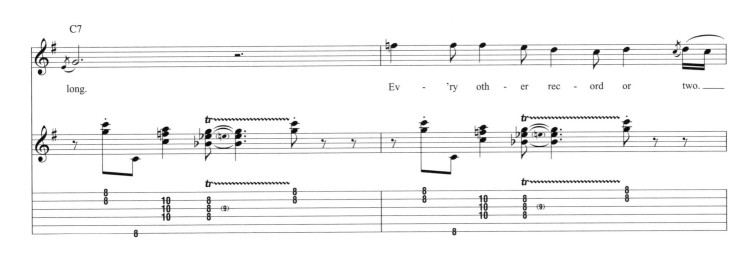

All she want-ed to hear was these down home blues all night

long. Ev - 'ry oth - er rec - ord or two.

Fade out

First Time I Met the Blues

Written by Eurreal "Little Brother" Montgomery

© 1960 (Renewed 1988) FLOMONT MUSIC (BMI) and ARC MUSIC CORP.
All Rights for FLOMONT MUSIC Controlled and Administered by BUG MUSIC, INC., A BMG CHRYSALIS COMPANY
All Rights for ARC MUSIC CORP. Administered by BMG RIGHTS MANAGEMENT (US) LLC
All Rights outside the U.S. Controlled by ARC MUSIC CORP.
All Rights Reserved   Used by Permission

the first time, __ the first time I met the blues, blues, you know, I was walk-in', I was walk-in' down __ through the

woods. __

Yes, __

72

Going Down

Words and Music by Don Nix

Intro

Moderately slow ♩ = 84

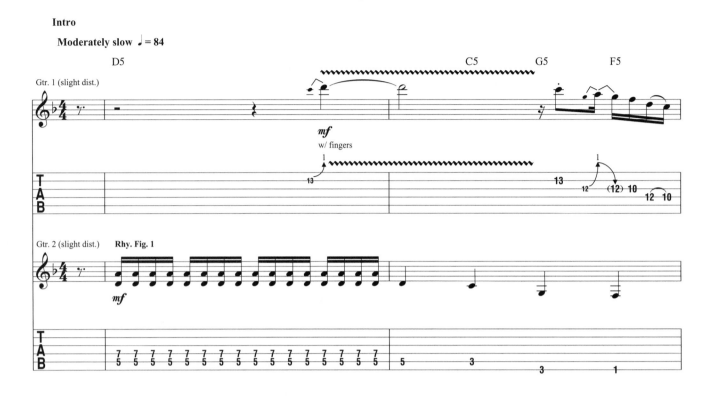

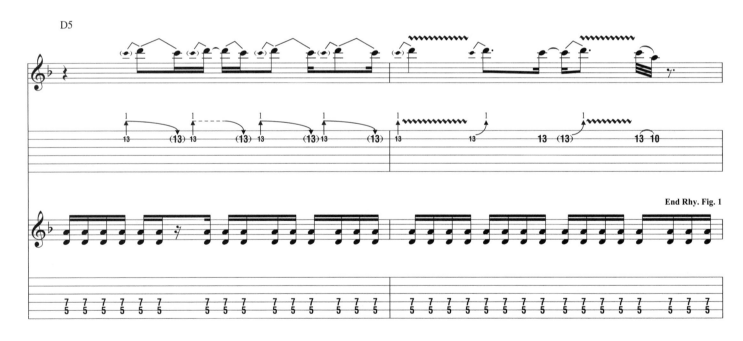

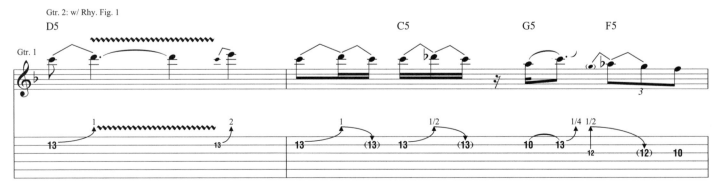

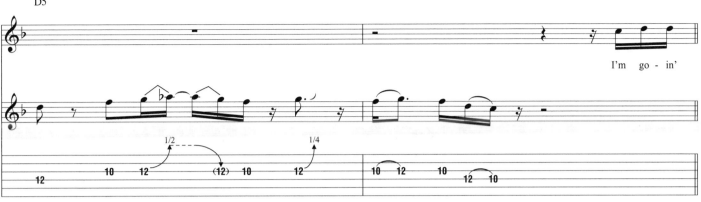

I'm go - in'

Chorus

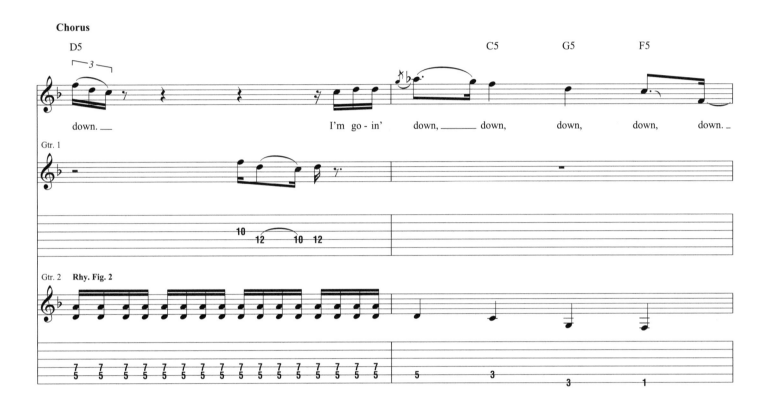

down. ___   I'm go - in'   down, ___ down,   down,   down,   down. __

Gtr. 1

Gtr. 2   **Rhy. Fig. 2**

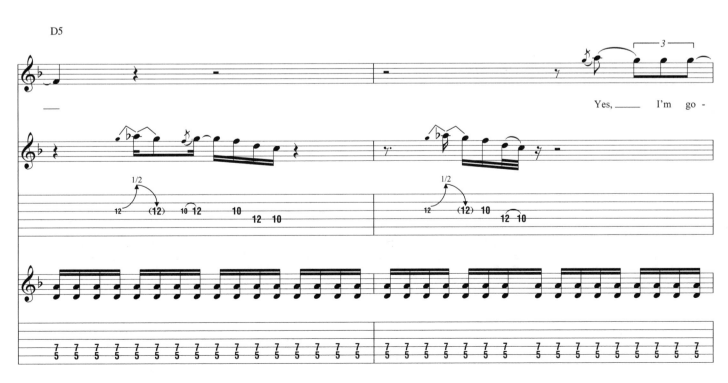

___   Yes, ___   I'm go -

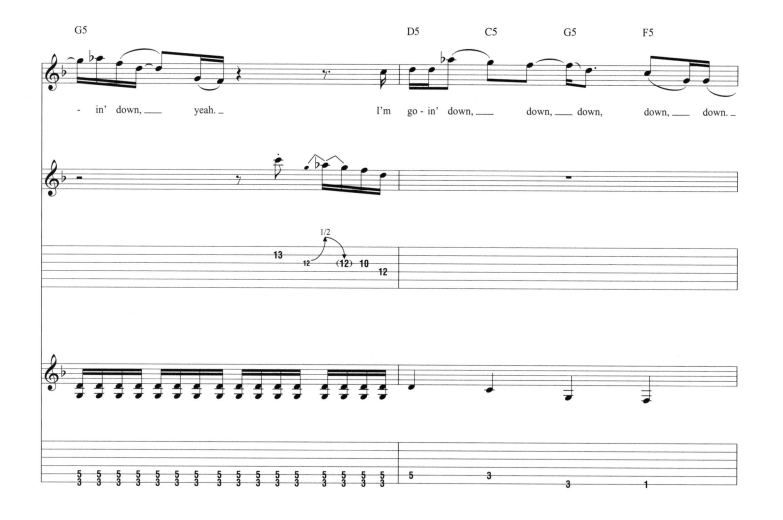

- in' down, ____ yeah. ____ I'm go - in' down, ____ down, ____ down, ____ down, ____ down. ____

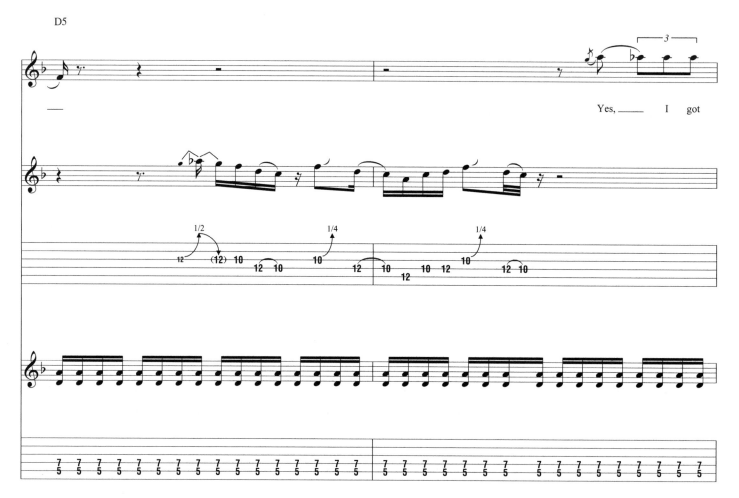

____ Yes, ____ I got

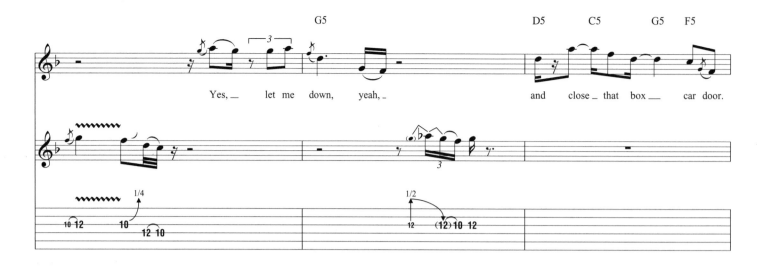

Yes, __ let me down, yeah, __ and close __ that box __ car door.

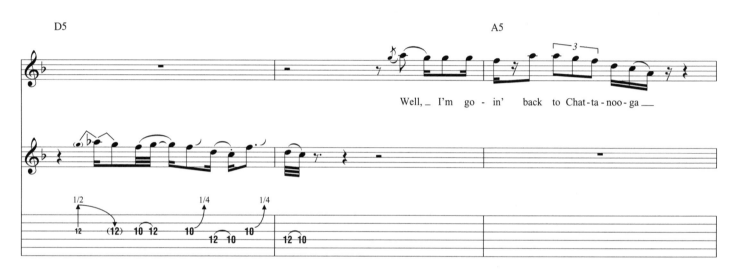

Well, __ I'm go - in' back to Chat - ta - noo - ga __

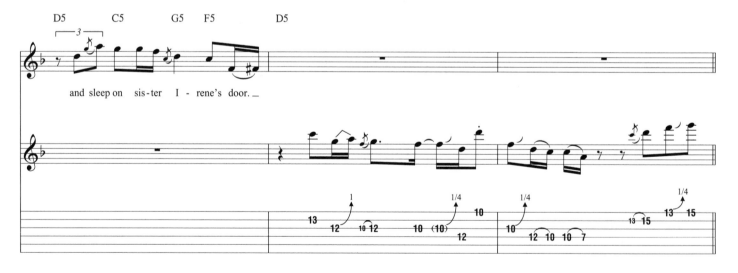

and sleep on sis - ter I - rene's door. __

Guitar Solo

Gtr. 2: w/ Rhy. Fig. 2

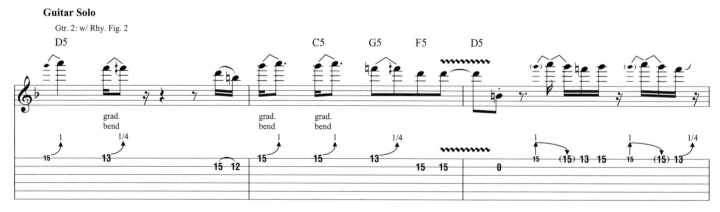

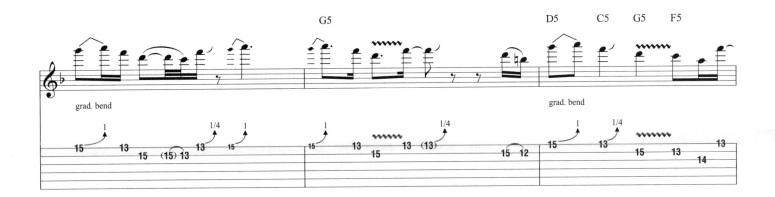

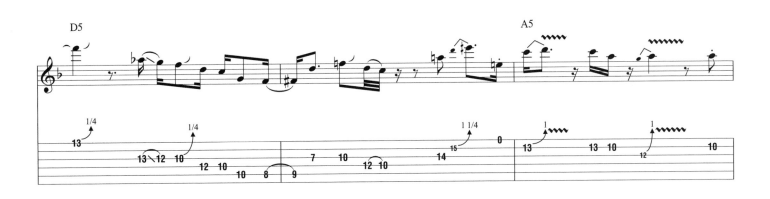

Chorus

Gtr. 2: w/ Rhy. Fig. 2

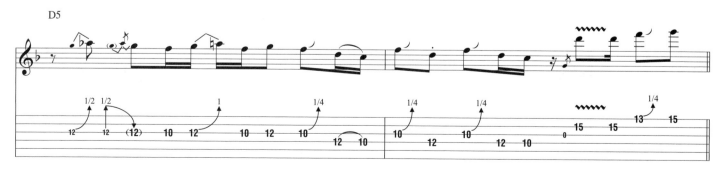

Outro-Guitar Solo

Gtr. 2: w/ Rhy. Fig. 2 (till fade)

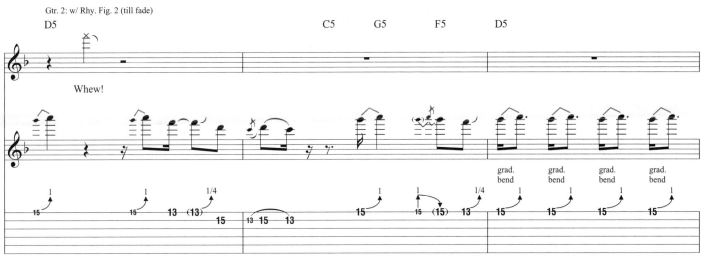

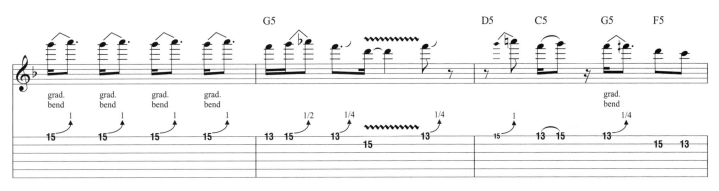

Begin fade

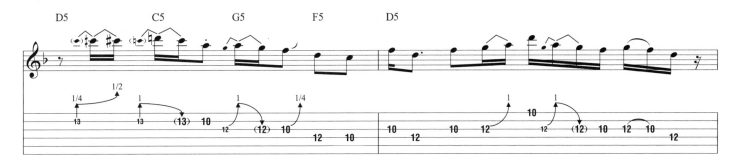

Fade out

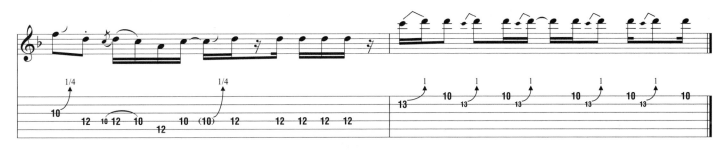

from Albert Collins - *Cold Snap*

I Ain't Drunk

Words and Music by Jimmie Liggins

Gtr. 2: Open Fm tuning, capo IV:
(low to high) F-C-F-Ab-C-F

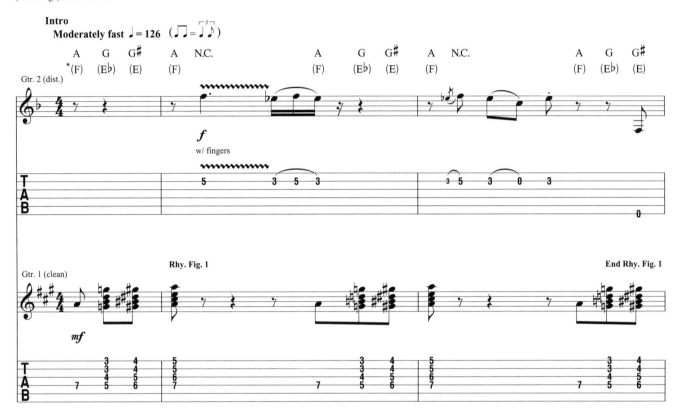

*Symbols in parentheses represent chord names respective to capoed guitar. Symbols above represent
actual sounding chords. Capoed fret is "0" in tab. Chord symbols reflect overall harmony.

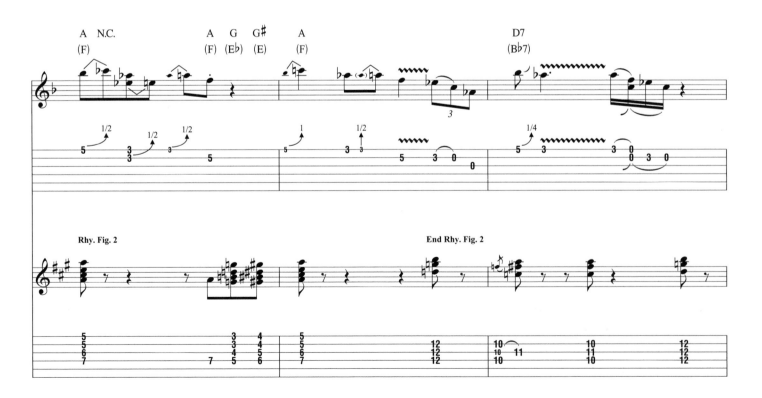

*T = Thumb on 6th string

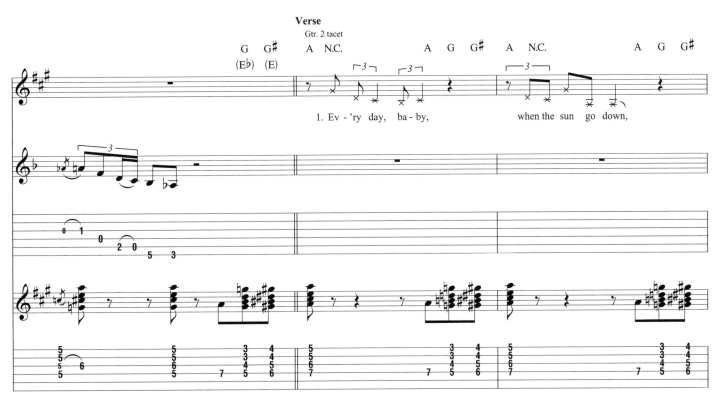

Verse

Gtr. 2 tacet

1. Ev-'ry day, ba-by, when the sun go down,

Chorus

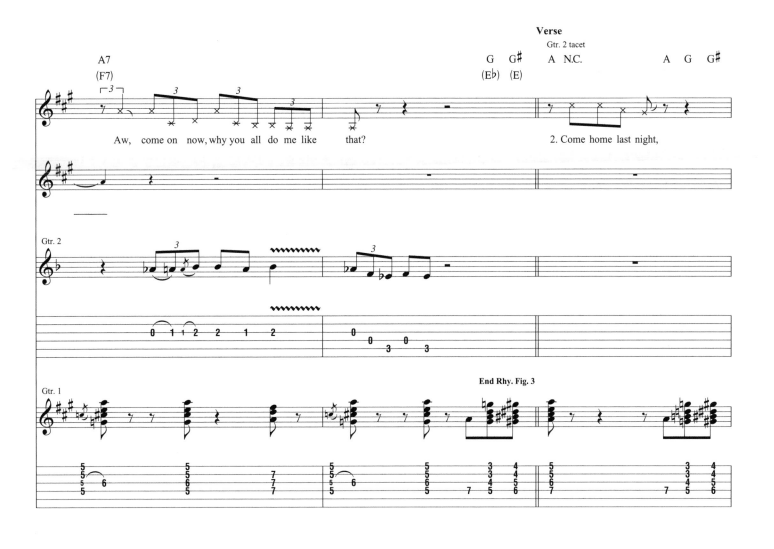

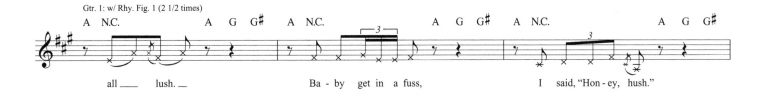

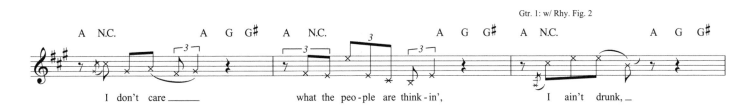

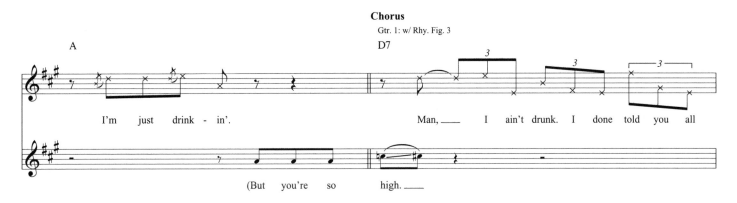

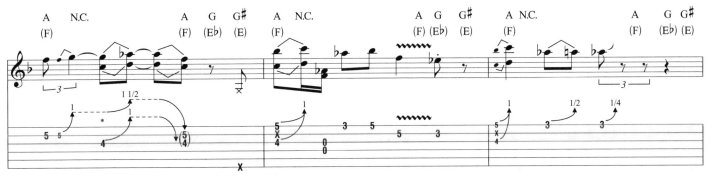

*3rd string caught by bend on 2nd string; don't pick.

Gtr. 1: w/ Rhy. Fig. 2

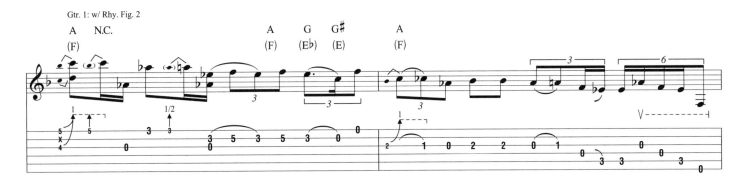

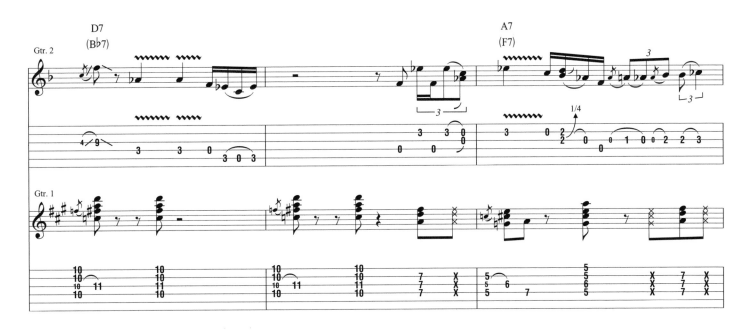

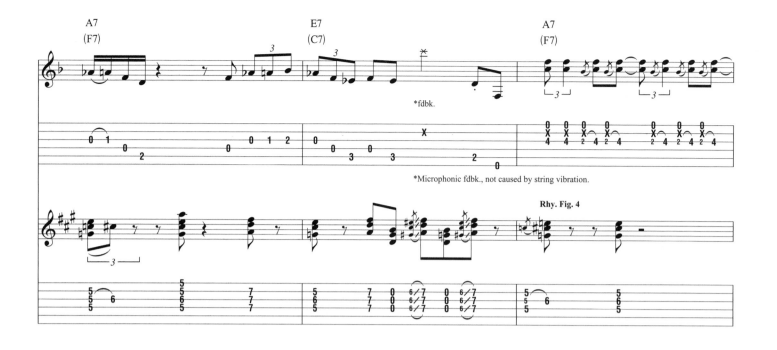

*Microphonic fdbk., not caused by string vibration.

Rhy. Fig. 4

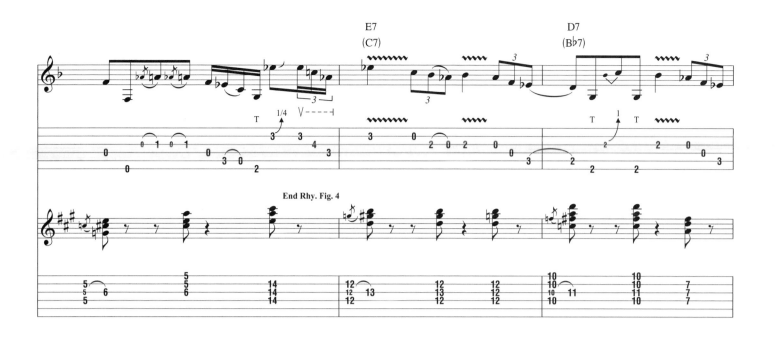

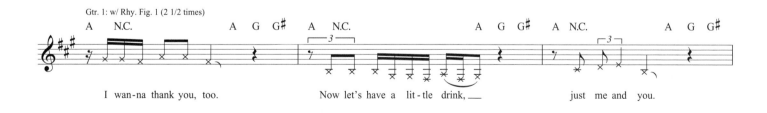

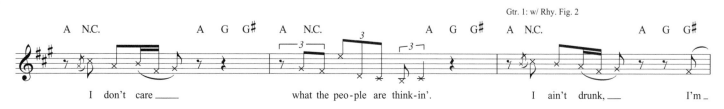

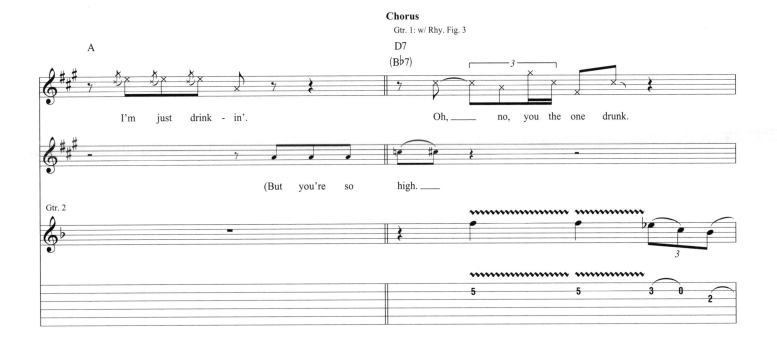

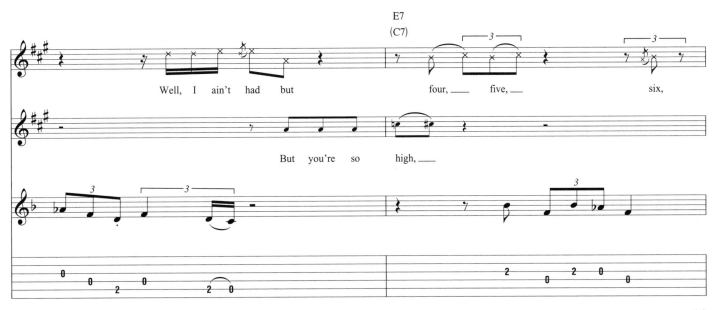

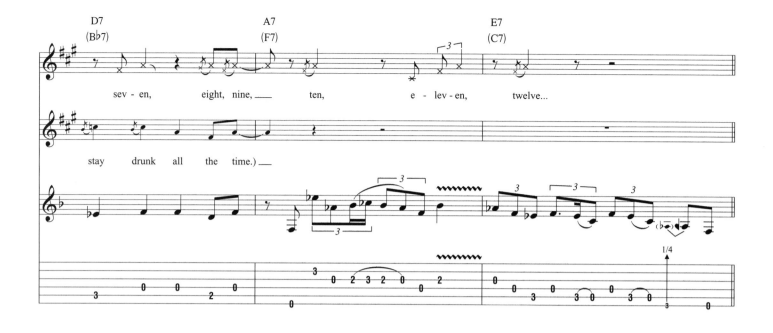

seven, eight, nine, ____ ten, e - lev - en, twelve...

stay drunk all the time.) ____

Outro-Guitar Solo
Gtr. 1: w/ Rhy. Fig. 4 (1st 7 meas.)

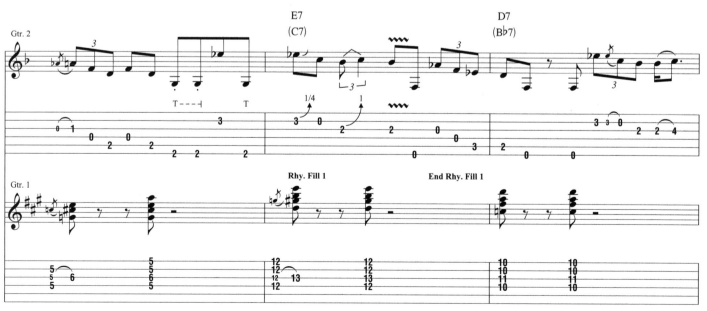

from Michael Burks - *I Smell Smoke*

I Smell Smoke

Words and Music by Sally Tiven, Jon Tiven and Roger Reale

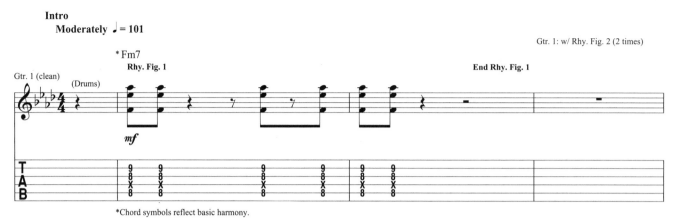

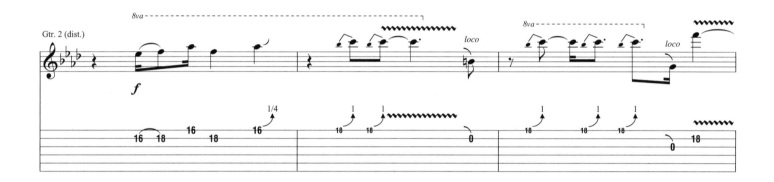

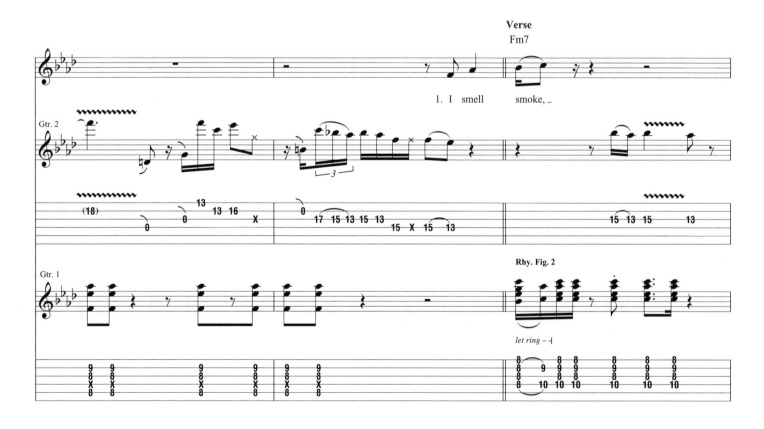

you must be burn - ing me ___ be-hind ___ my back. ___

I smell

smoke,

you must be burn - ing me ___ be-hind ___ my back.

I smell

Chorus

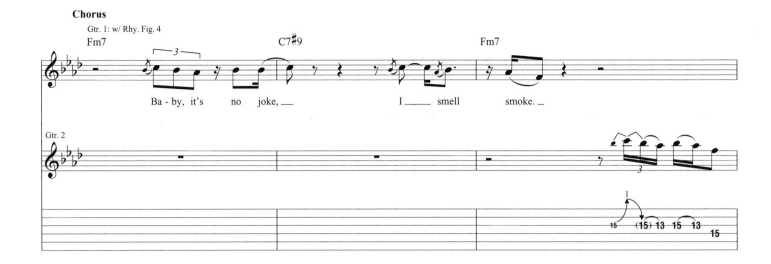

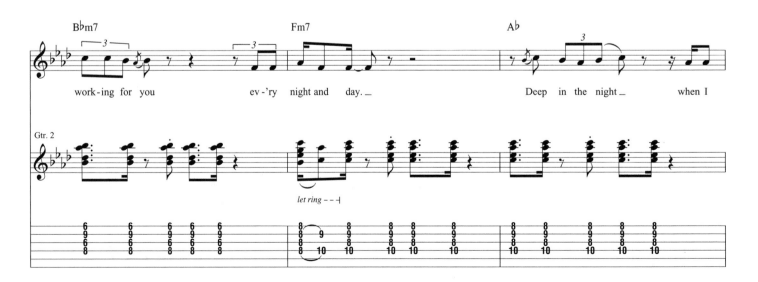

turn to you, ____ I feel my worst fears have __ come _ true. ____

Organ Solo

Gtr. 1: w/ Rhy. Fig. 2

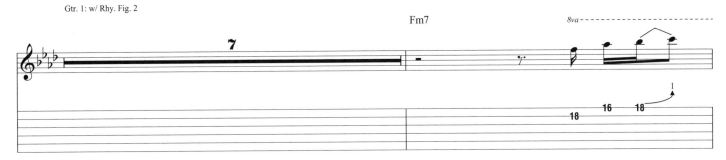

Guitar Solo

Gtr. 1: w/ Rhy. Fig. 3

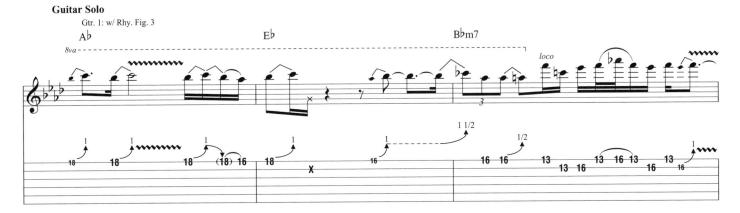

Gtr. 1: w/ Rhy. Fig. 4

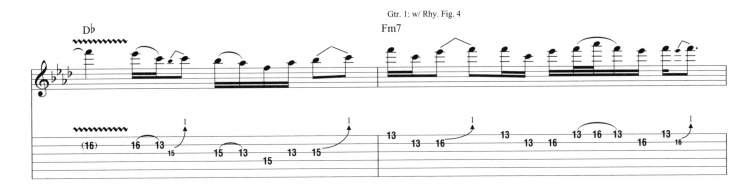

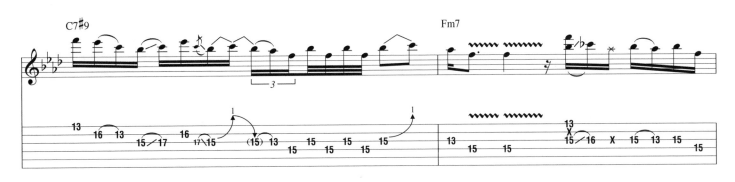

Bridge

I smell smoke, when you think you're a-lone and there's no-bod - y look-

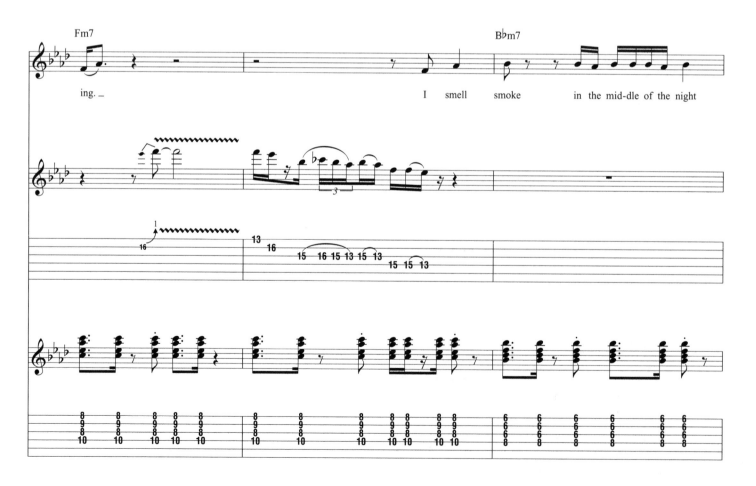

ing. ___ I smell smoke in the mid-dle of the night

Fm7

When I know no - bod - y's cook - ing.

let ring

Pre-Chorus
Gtr. 1: w/ Rhy. Fig. 5
Gtr. 2 tacet

A♭   E♭   B♭m7

You can play it down and hide it with per - fume, I smell some - thing burn - ing when you

Chorus
Gtr. 1: w/ Rhy. Fig. 4 (1st 2 meas.)

D♭   Fm7   C7♯9

walk in - to the room. Yeah, it's no joke. I smell

Gtr. 2

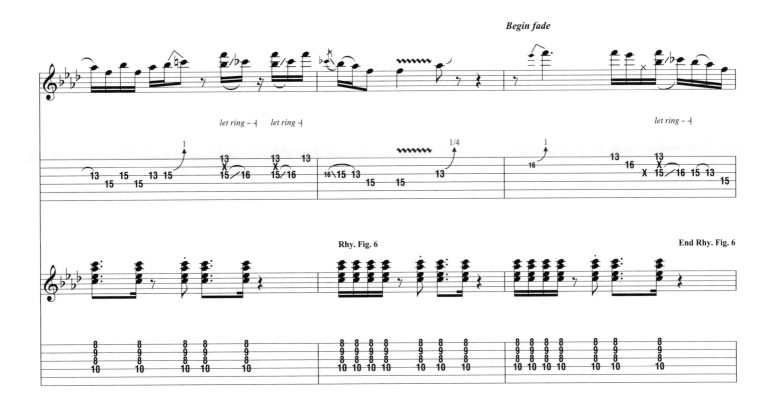

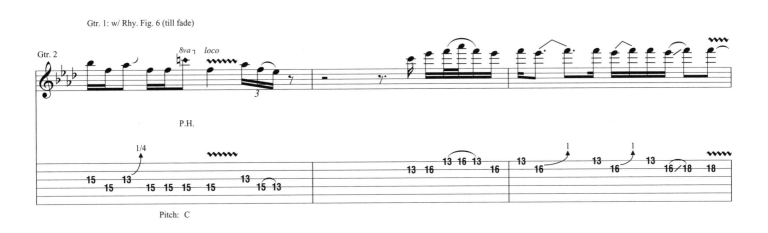

I'm Yours and I'm Hers

Words and Music by Johnny Winter

*Chord symbols reflect overall harmony.

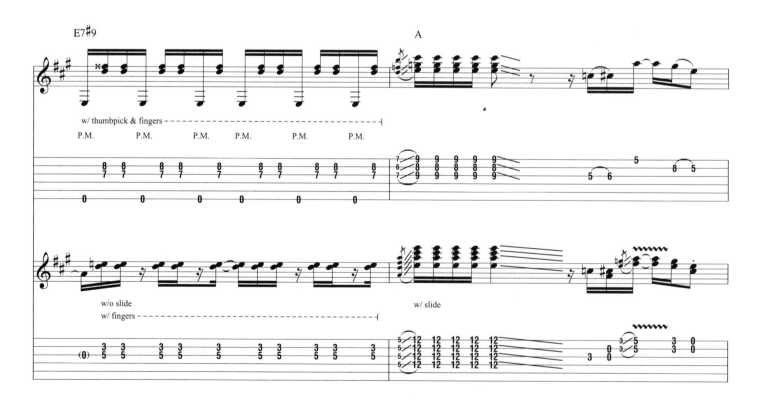

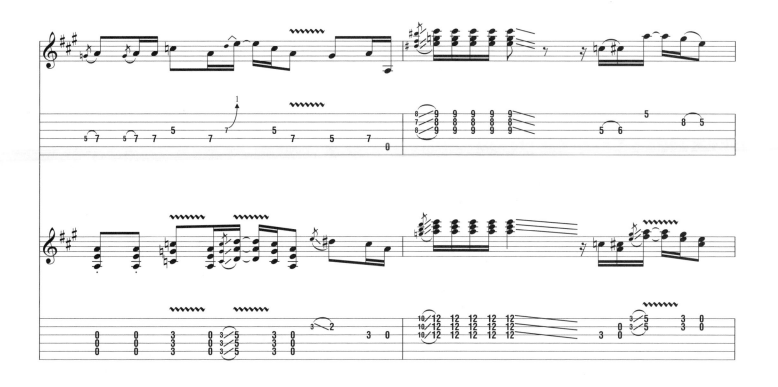

Verse

A

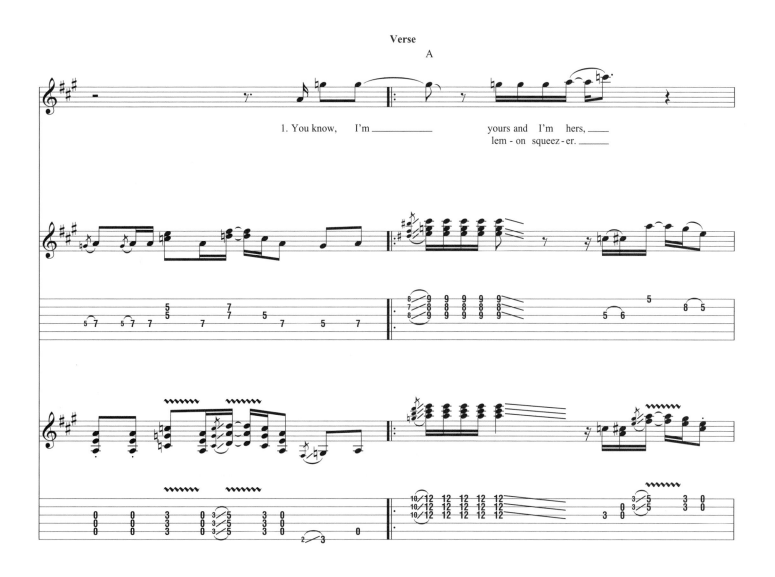

1. You know, I'm _____ yours and I'm hers, _____
lem - on squeez - er. _____

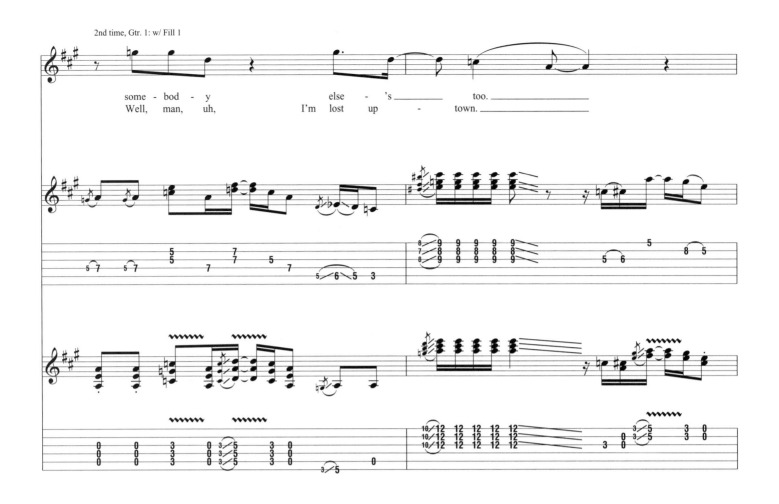

some - bod - y   else - 's _____ too. _____
Well, man, uh,   I'm lost up - town. _____

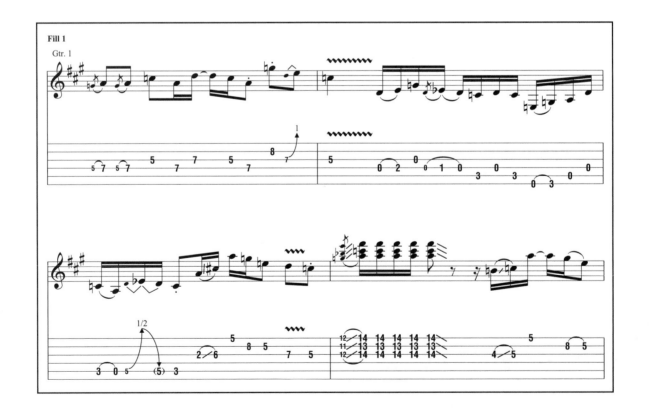

Fill 1

Gtr. 1

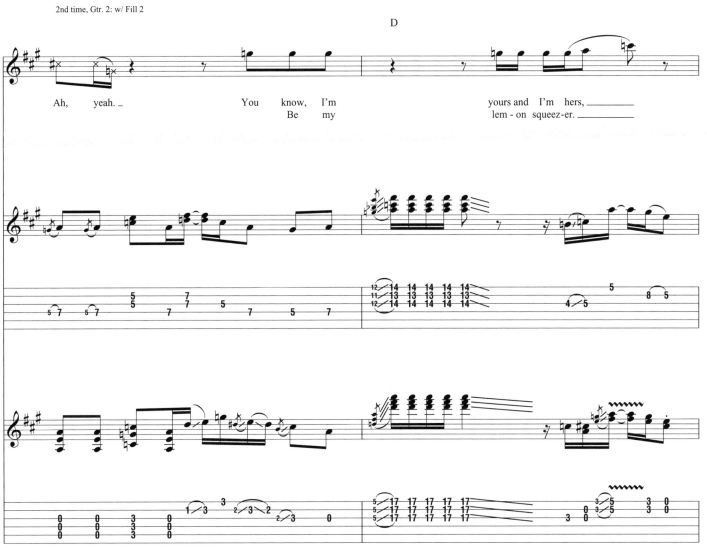

Ah,   yeah. _

You   know,   I'm
Be   my

yours and   I'm   hers, _____
lem - on squeez-er. _____

Fill 2

Gtr. 2

let ring - - - - ┤

w/ slide

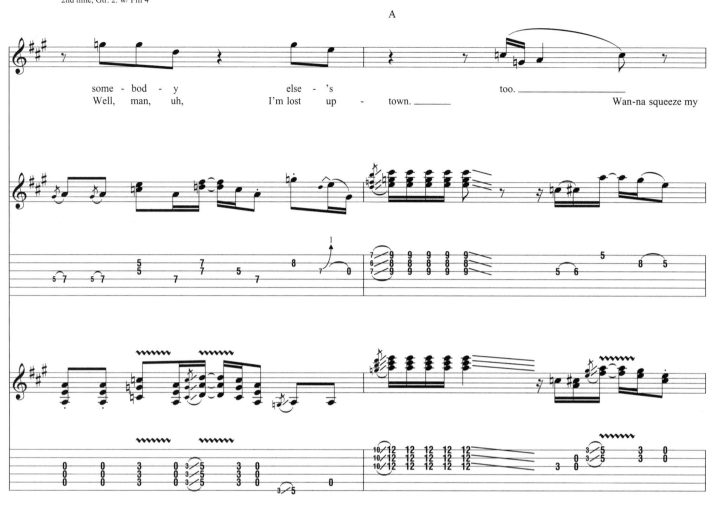

some - bod - y   else - 's   too. _____
Well, man, uh,   I'm lost up - town. _____   Wan-na squeeze my

Fill 3

Gtr. 1

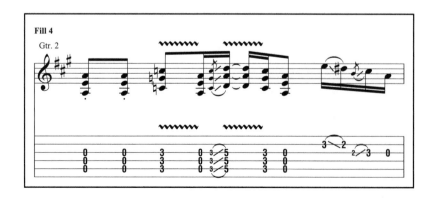

Fill 4

Gtr. 2

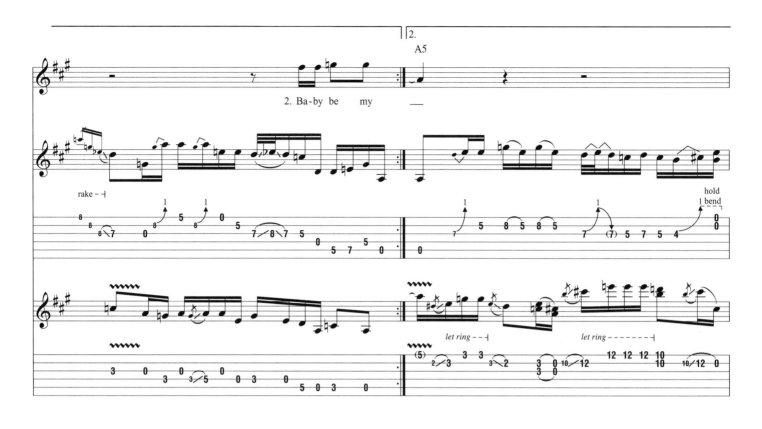

2. Ba-by be my

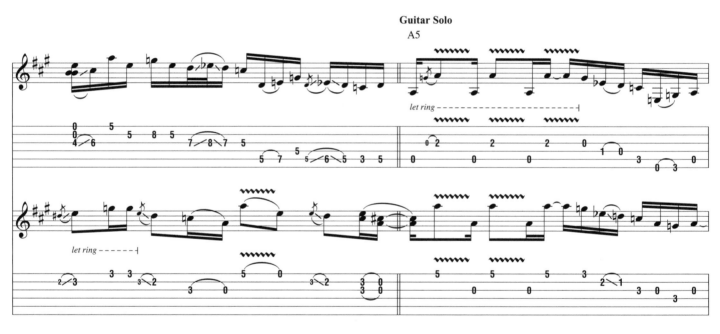

Guitar Solo

A5

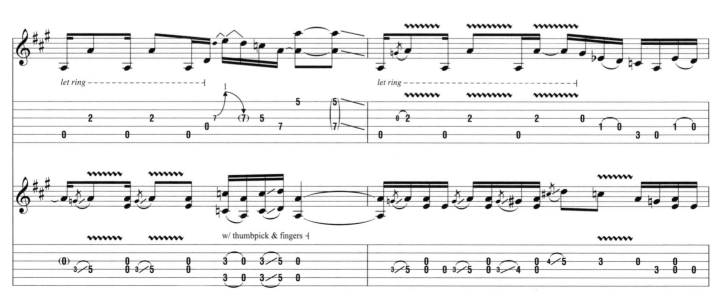

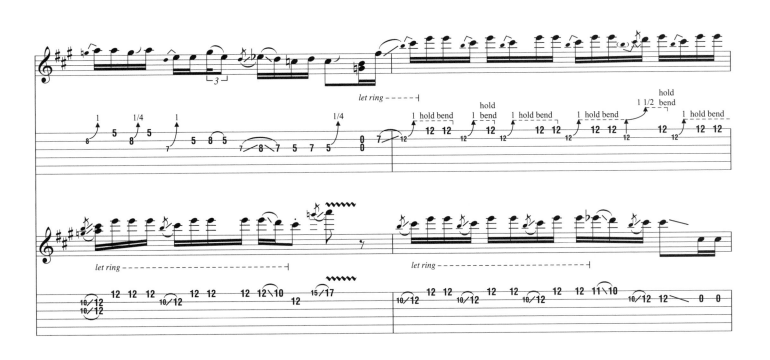

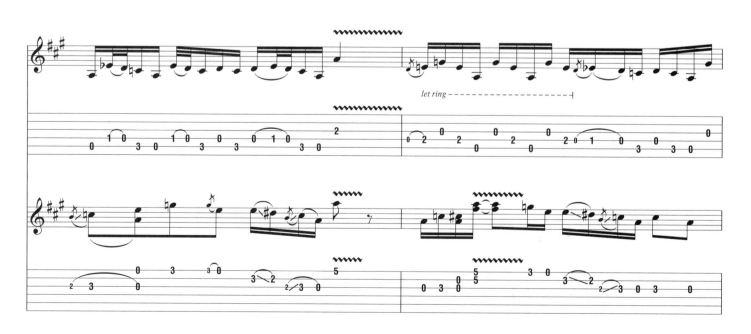

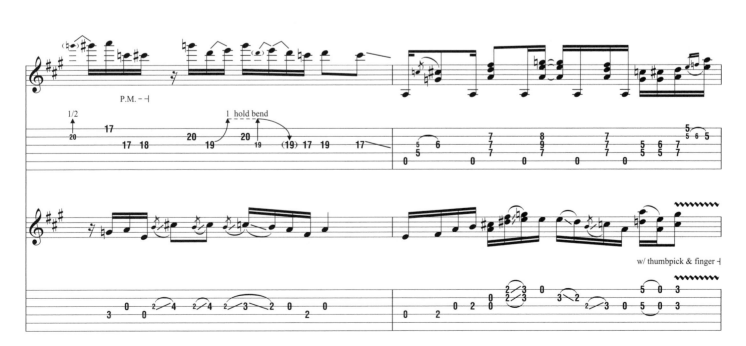

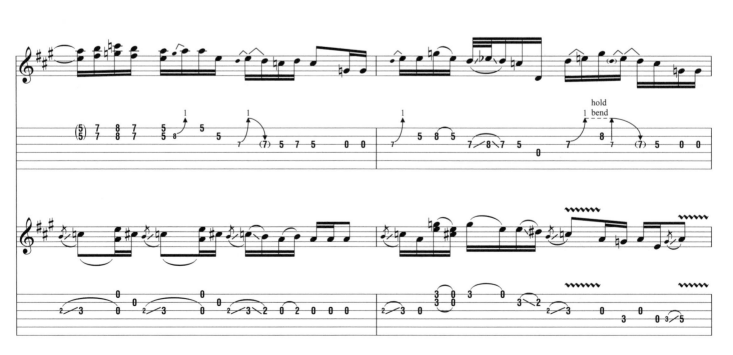

114

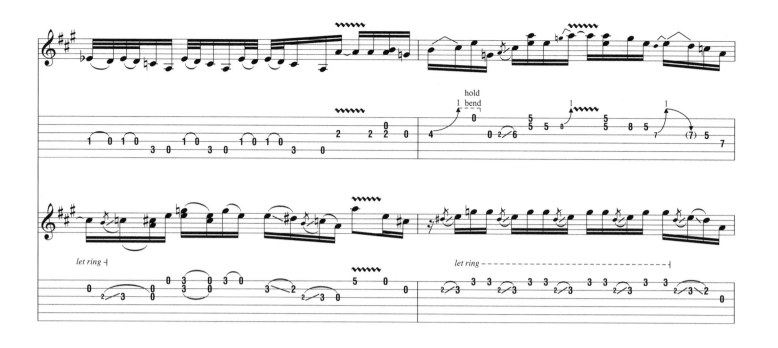

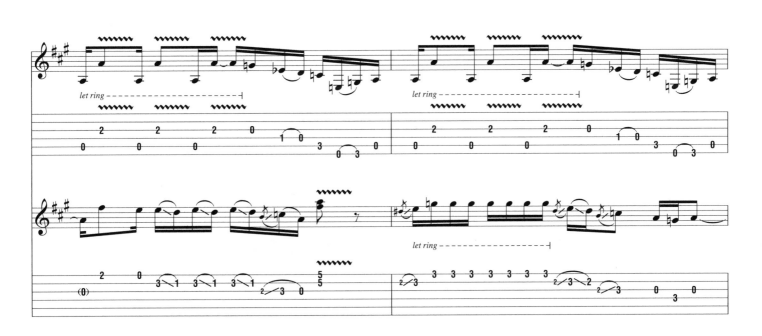

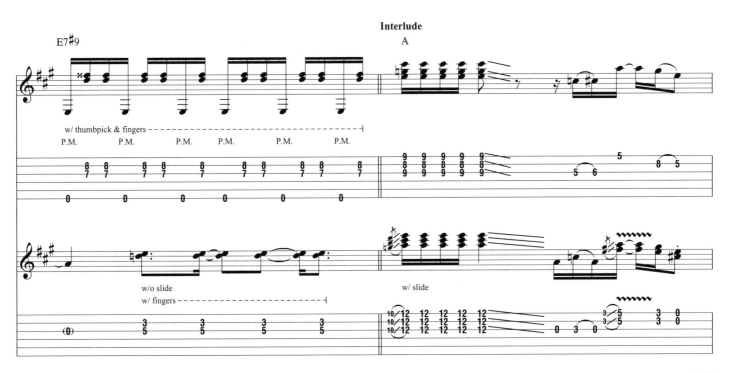

Verse

A

3. Want to _____ take you with me, _____

let ring - - - - -

want you all to un - der - stand. _____ Ah, _____

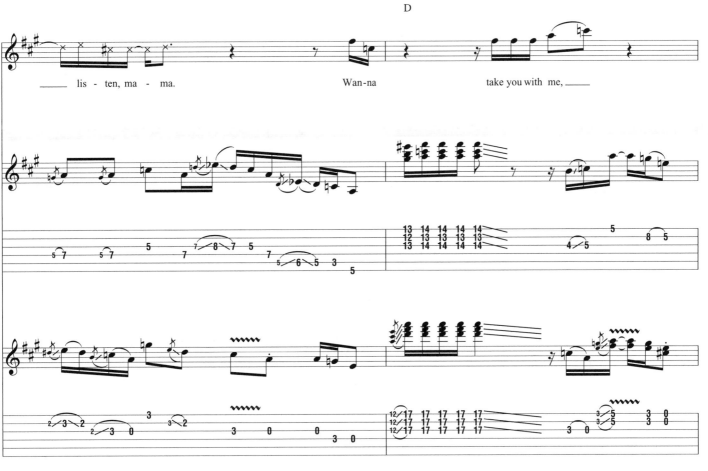

lis - ten, ma - ma.   Wan-na   take you with me, _____

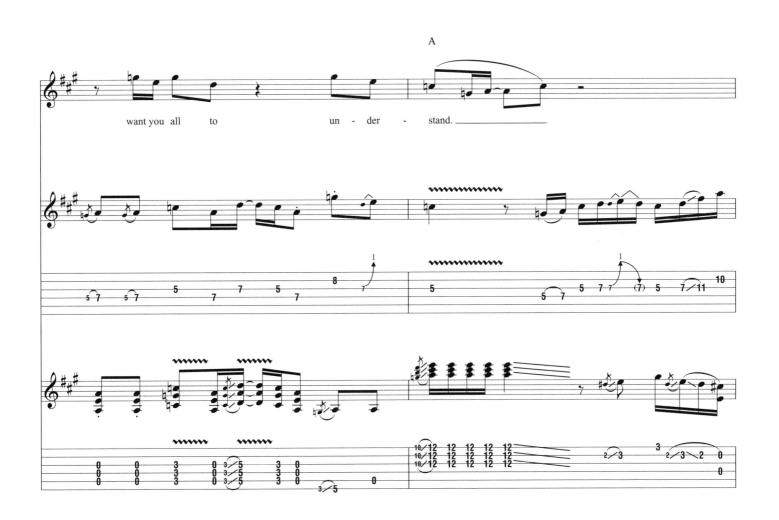

want you all to un - der - stand. _____

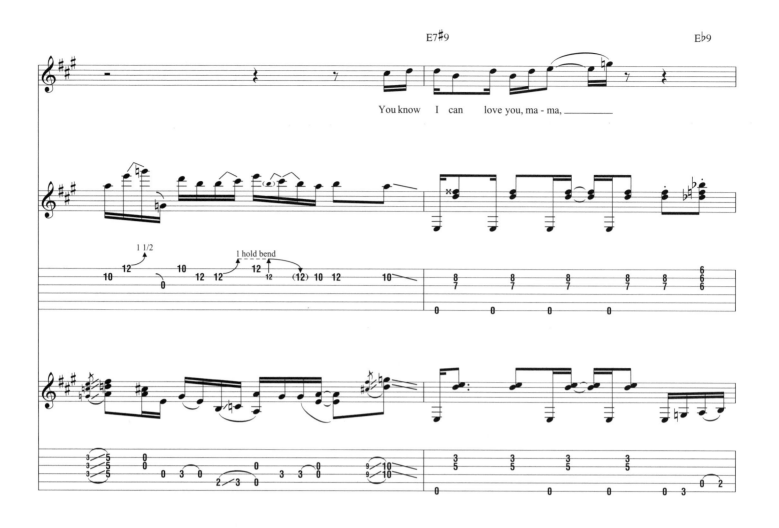

You know   I   can   love you, ma - ma, _____

bet - ter   than   your _____   stead - y   man. _____

121

from Susan Tedeschi - *Just Won't Burn*

It Hurt So Bad

Words and Music by Tom Hambridge

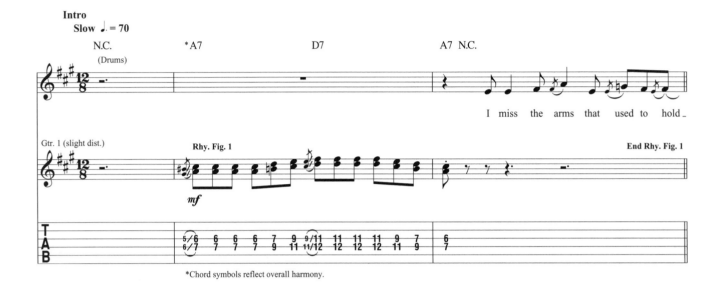

*Chord symbols reflect overall harmony.

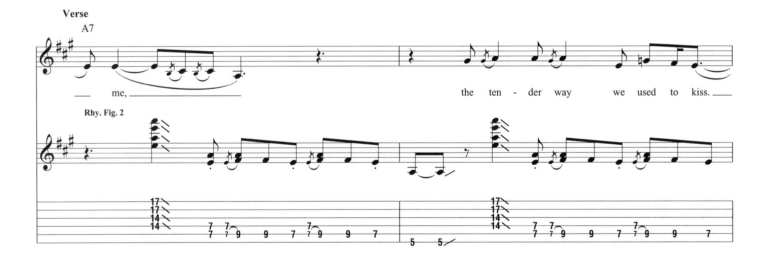

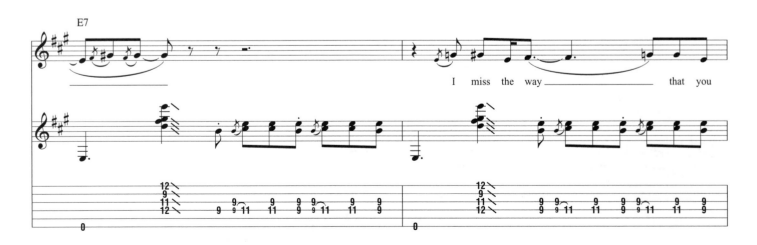

Chorus

bad, _____ you are the best man __ I ev-

-er had, _____ why was I so __ blind _____

___ to see? _____ Now the big-gest fool _____ is

me. _____ 3. I miss the arms that used _____

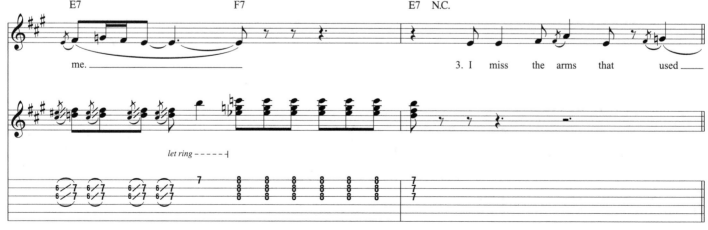

let ring - - - - -

124

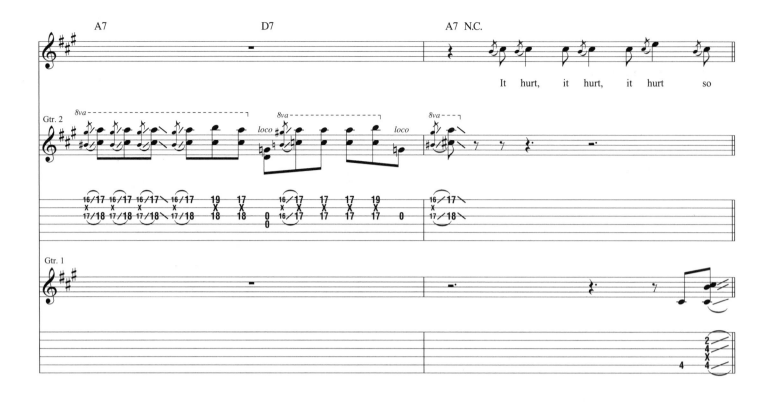

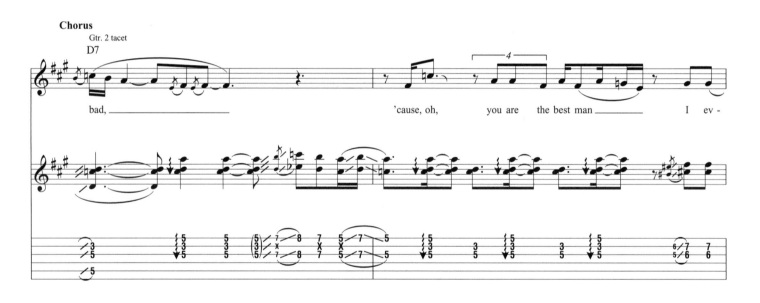

to see? And now the big-gest fool __ is

me. __ 4. Oh, __ oh, __ what a fool I was, dar - lin', __ yes, __

Verse

and, oh, you were a fool to let, __

let __ me go, __ why __ did you let __ me go? It's so lone - some here __

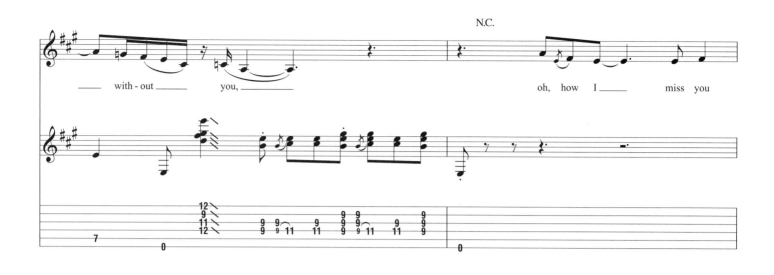

with - out _____ you, _____ oh, how I _____ miss you

so. _____ Oh, oh, now, _____

Outro
Gtr. 1: w/ Rhy. Fig. 1 (4 times)

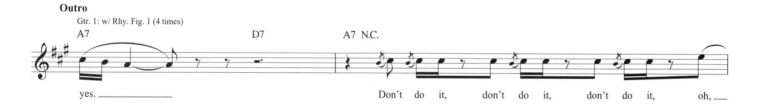

yes. _____ Don't do it, don't do it, don't do it, oh, _____

_____ Lord, no. I miss you, _____ oh, _____

_____ yeah. Come back, _____ oh, _____ come back _____

_____ to me, yes. Oh, how _____ I

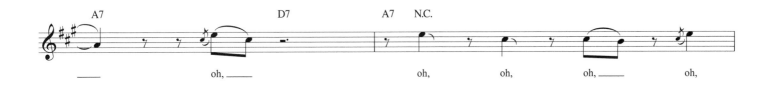

from Rory Gallagher - *Rory Gallagher*

Laundromat

Words and Music by Rory Gallagher

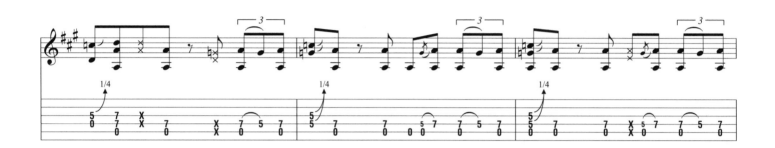

*Chord symbols reflect implied harmony.

don't have no clothes ___ to clean, ___ to put in - side ___ the ma -

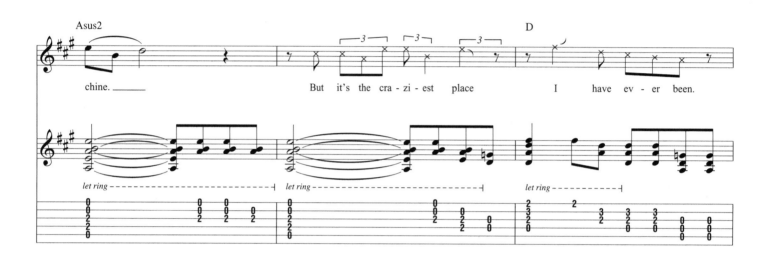

chine. ___ But it's the cra - zi - est place I have ev - er been.

Chorus

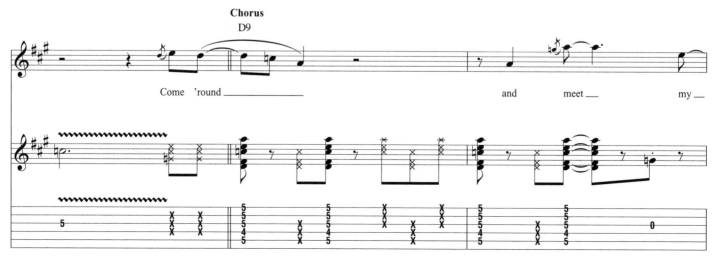

Come 'round ___ and meet ___ my ___

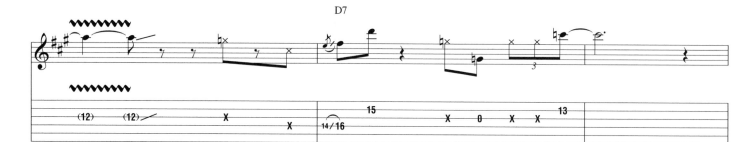

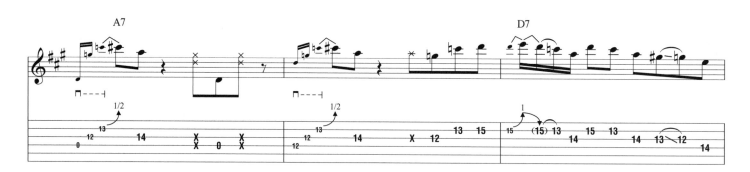

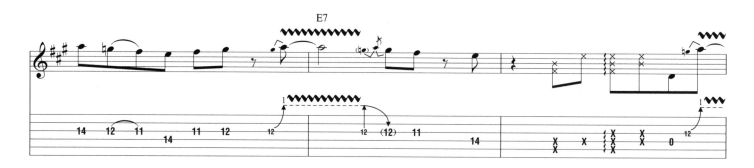

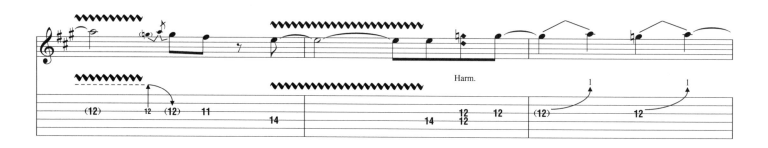

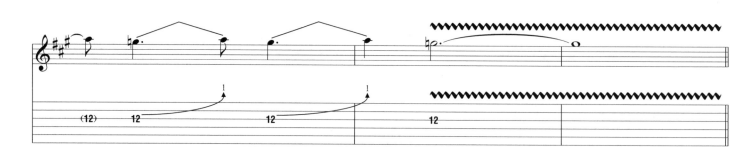

Interlude

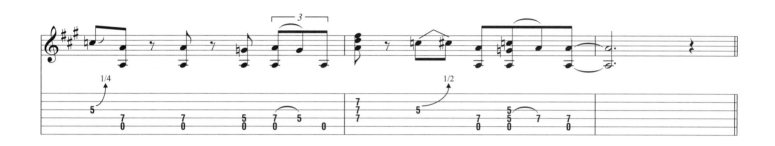

Verse

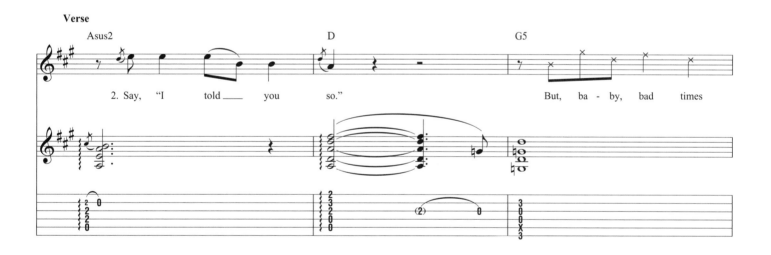

2. Say, "I told ___ you so." But, ba - by, bad times

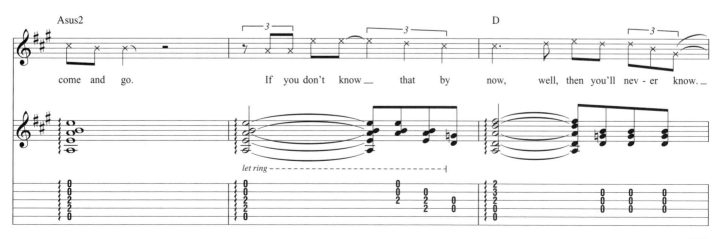

come and go. If you don't know ___ that by now, well, then you'll nev - er know. ___

Interlude

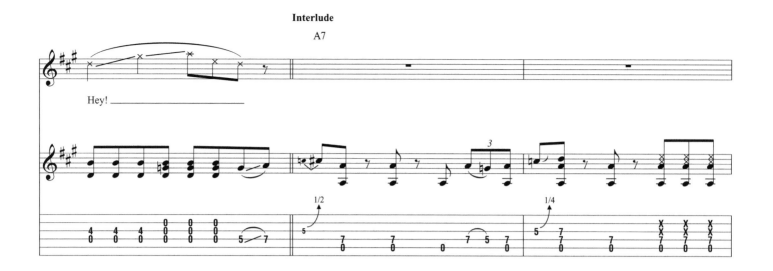

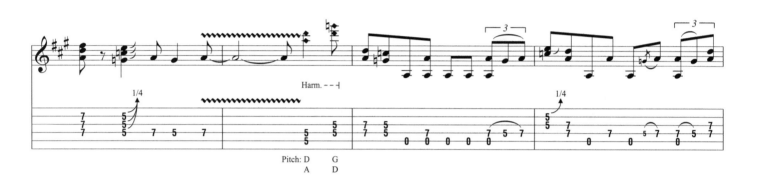

Verse

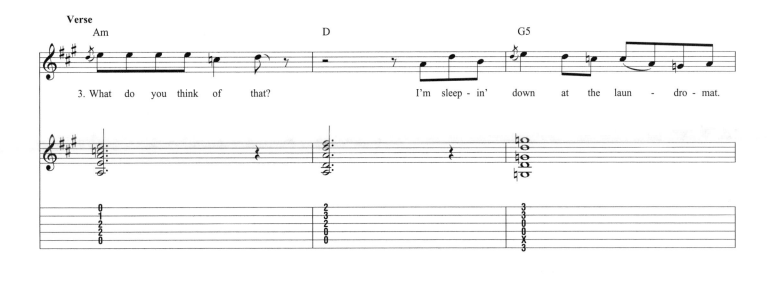

3. What do you think of that?   I'm sleep-in' down at the laun - dro - mat.

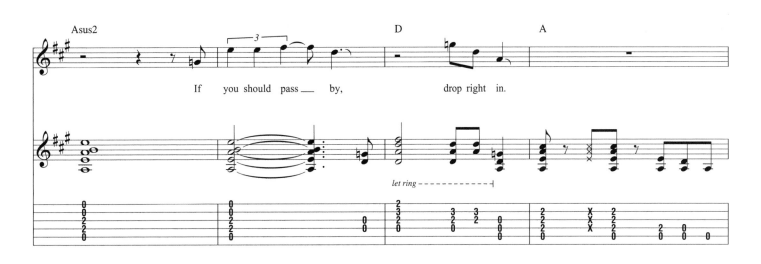

If   you should pass ___ by,   drop right in.

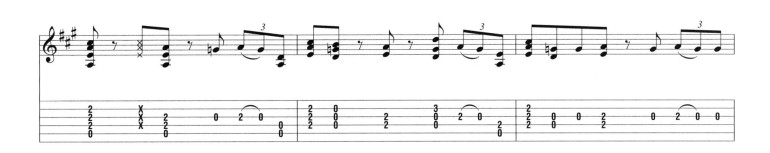

Well, I don't ___ have no clothes ___ to

They'll be there with me, ___

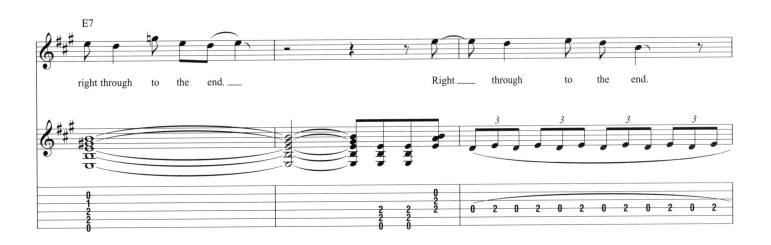

right through to the end. ___

Right ___ through to the end.

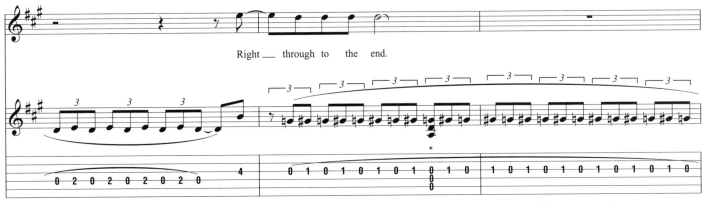

Right ___ through to the end.

*Strum open 4th & 5th strings while executing pull-off.

Interlude

A7

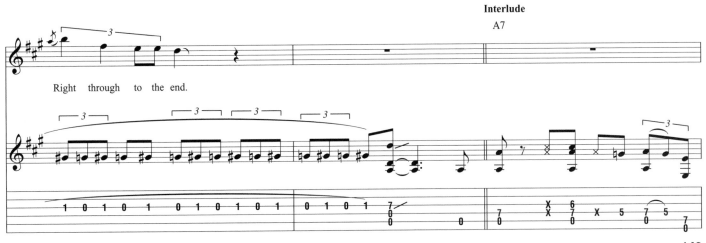

Right through to the end.

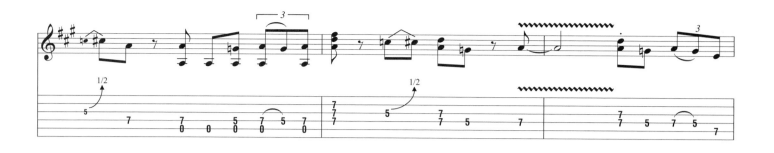

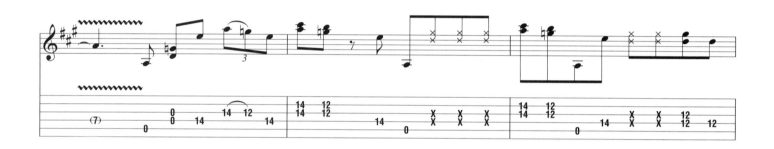

*Notes on 2nd string sound due to exaggerated vibrato on 3rd string.

let ring -

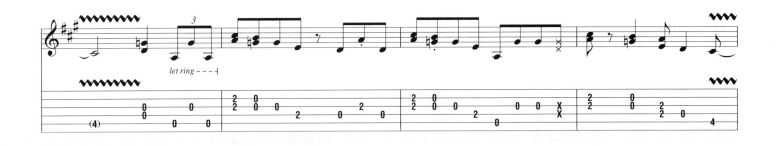

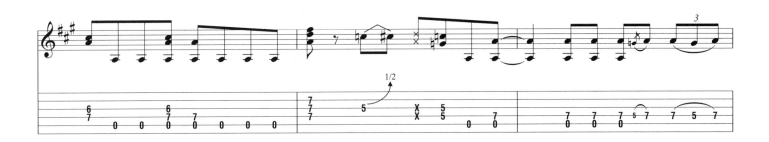

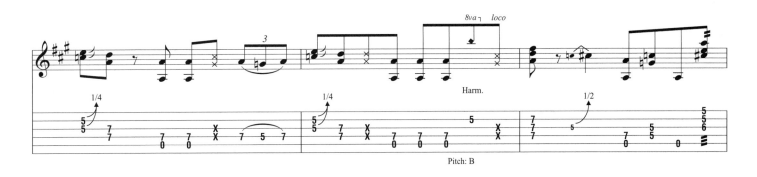

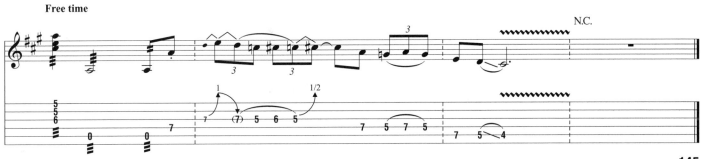

Laundromat Blues

Words and Music by Sandy Jones, Jr.

DGDGBE tuning, down 1 1/2 steps:
(low to high) B-E-B-E-G#-C#

Verse

Slow ♩. = 69

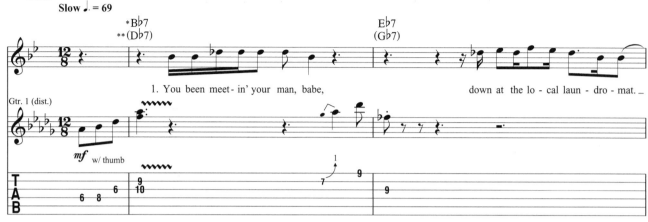

* Chord symbols reflect overall harmony.

** Symbols in parentheses represent chord names respective to detuned guitar. Symbols above reflect actual sounding chords.

up ear-ly ev-'ry morn - in' ___   and you grab your old blouse ___ or two. ___

Oh,   you

know you rush down ___ to the laun - dry ___

while your man is wait- in' on

you. ___

3. You

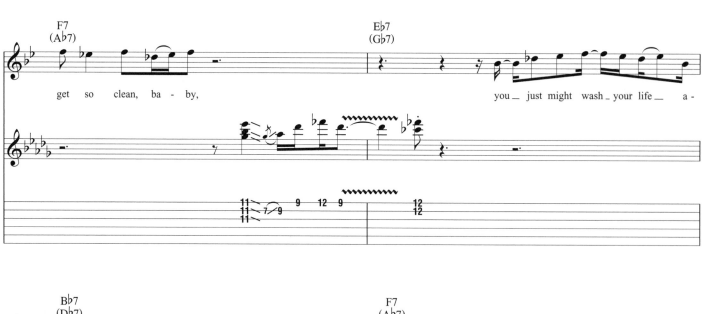

get so clean, ba - by, you just might wash your life a-

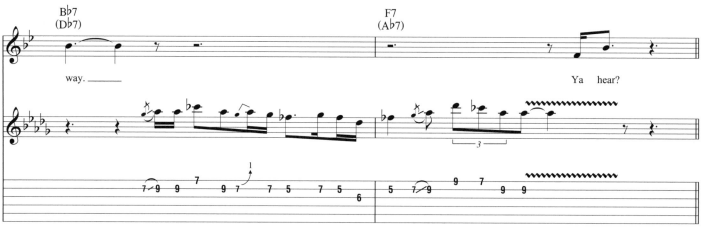

way. Ya hear?

Guitar Solo

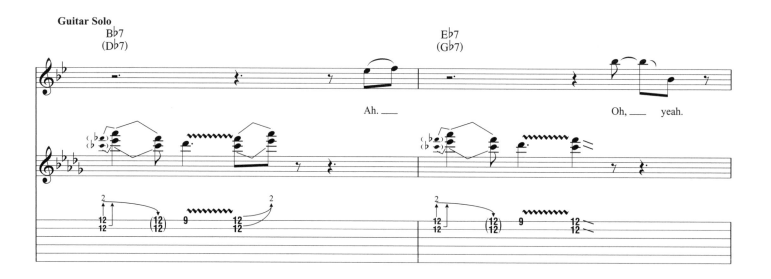

Ah. Oh, yeah.

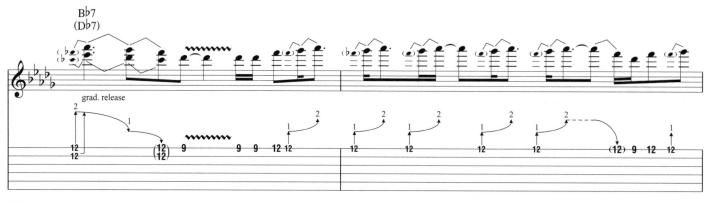

Well, all right. —

Ah! —

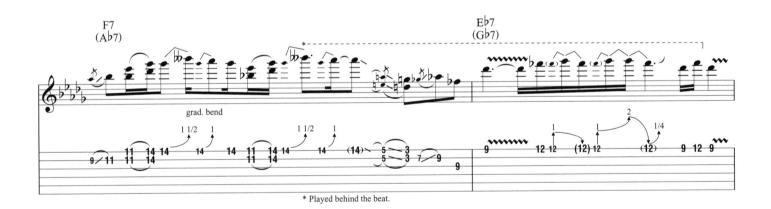

grad. bend

* Played behind the beat.

4. I know you

from Joe Bonamassa - *Blues Deluxe*

Long Distance Blues

Words and Music by Bernice Carter

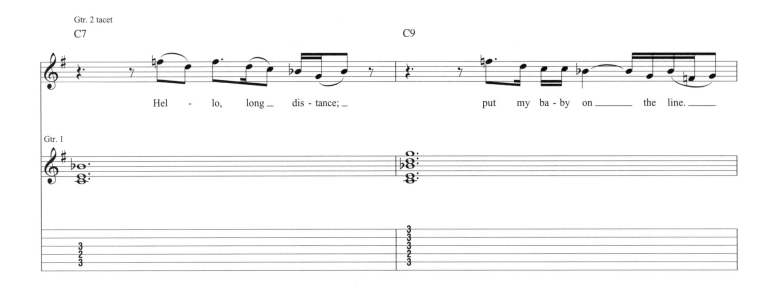

Gtr. 2 tacet

C7 · C9

Hel - lo, long _ dis - tance; _ put my ba - by on _____ the line. _____

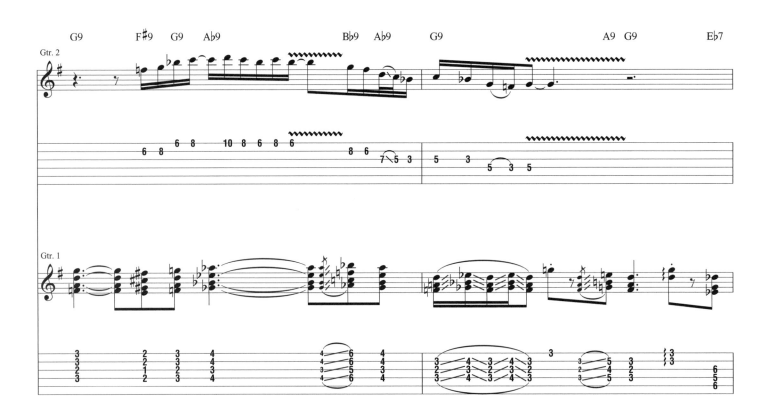

G9 · F#9 · G9 · Ab9 · · · · · · Bb9 · Ab9 · · G9 · · · · · · · · · A9 · G9 · · · · Eb7

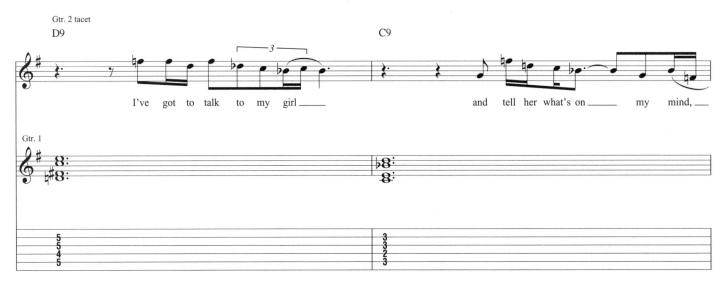

Gtr. 2 tacet

D9 · C9

I've got to talk to my girl _____ and tell her what's on _____ my mind, _____

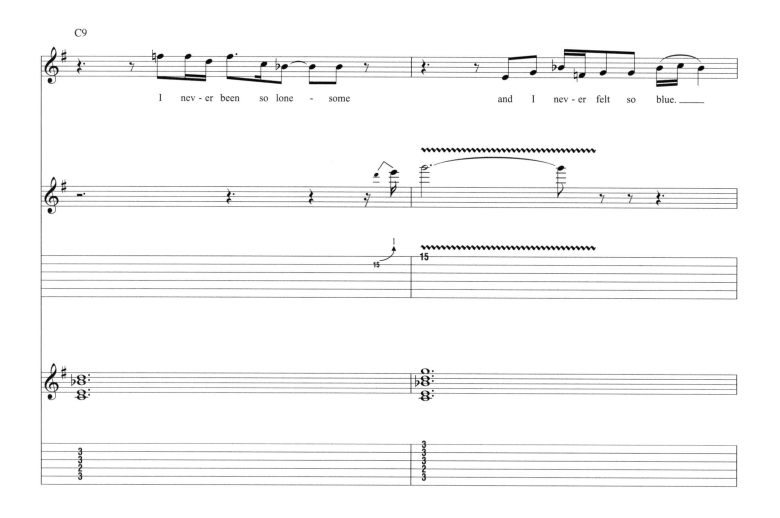

I nev-er been so lone - some   and I nev-er felt so blue. _____

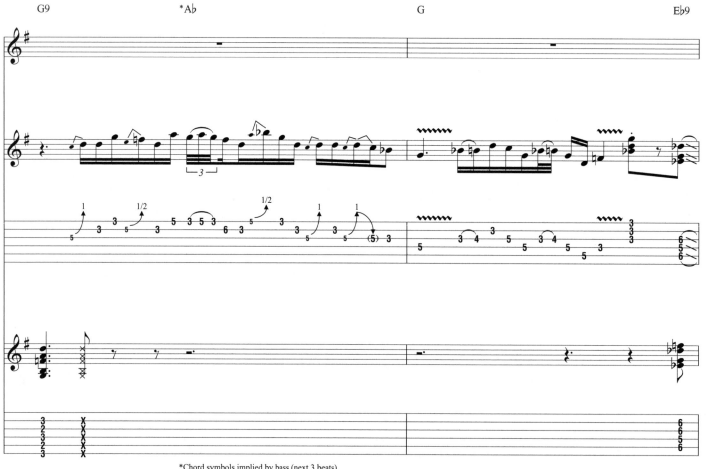

*Chord symbols implied by bass (next 3 beats).

Well, it's been a long time, __ ba - by, __ since I got a let - ter from you. __

Guitar Solo

Gtr. 1 tacet

Gtr. 2

*Chord symbols implied by bass (next 12 meas.).

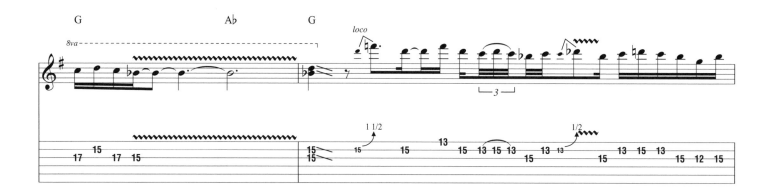

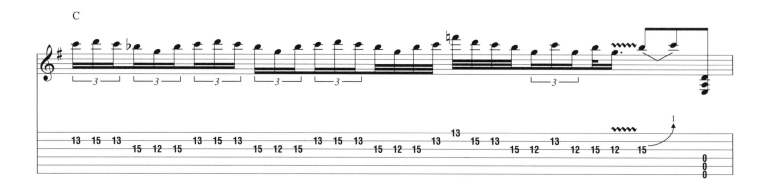

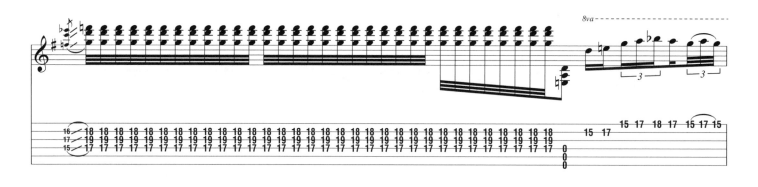

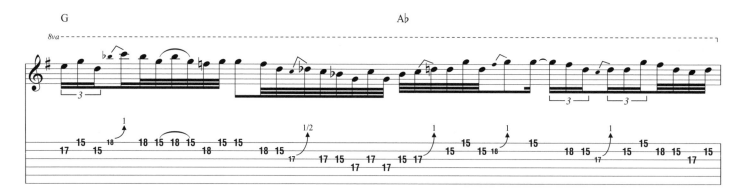

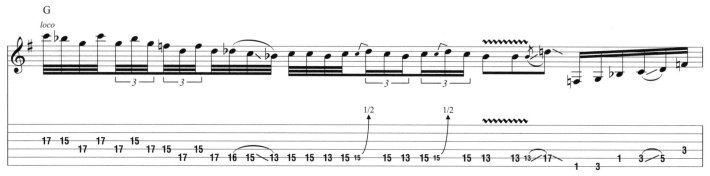

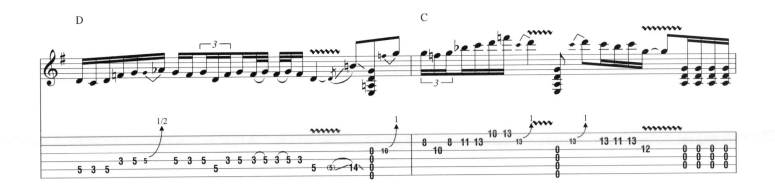

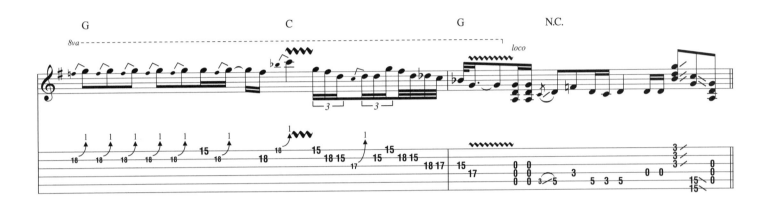

Verse

3. Send me some mon - ey, ba - by; please don't talk no trash. ____

What I learned ____ from you, dar - ling: less talk and a lot of cash. ____

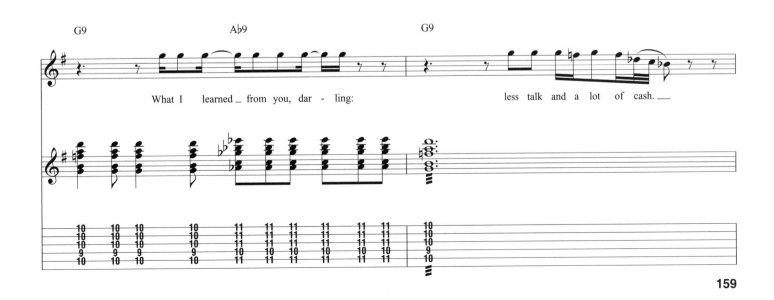

from Robben Ford - *Talk to Your Daughter*

Mama Talk to Your Daughter

Words and Music by J.B. Lenoir and Alex Atkins

Verse

Gtr. 1: w/Rhy. Fig. 1, 2¾ times

1. Ma - ma, pa - pa, please talk to your daugh - ter for me.

Ma - ma, pa - pa, please talk to your daugh - ter for me.

Gtr. 2 tacet

She done made me love her and I

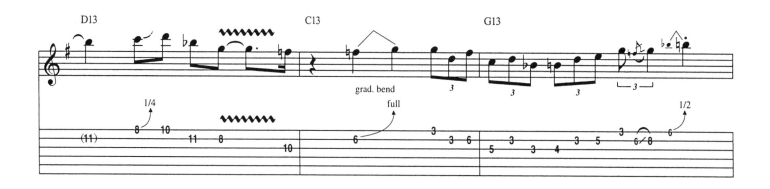

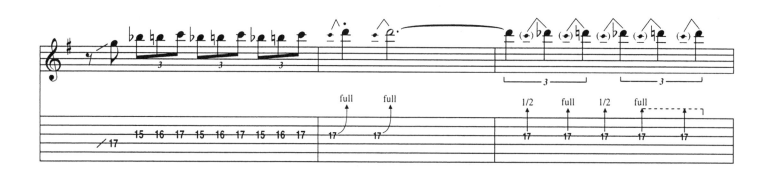

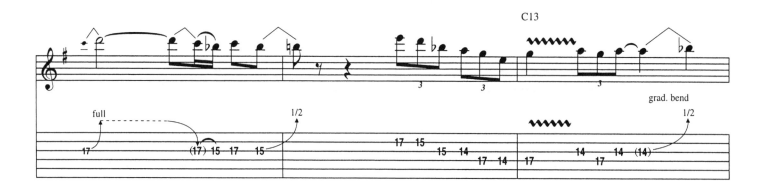

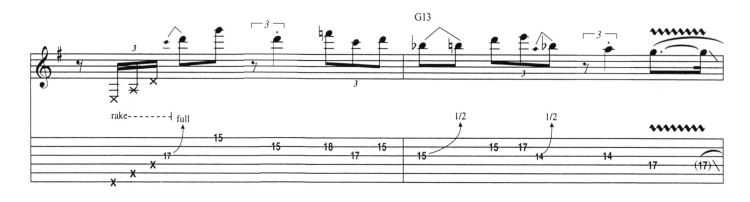

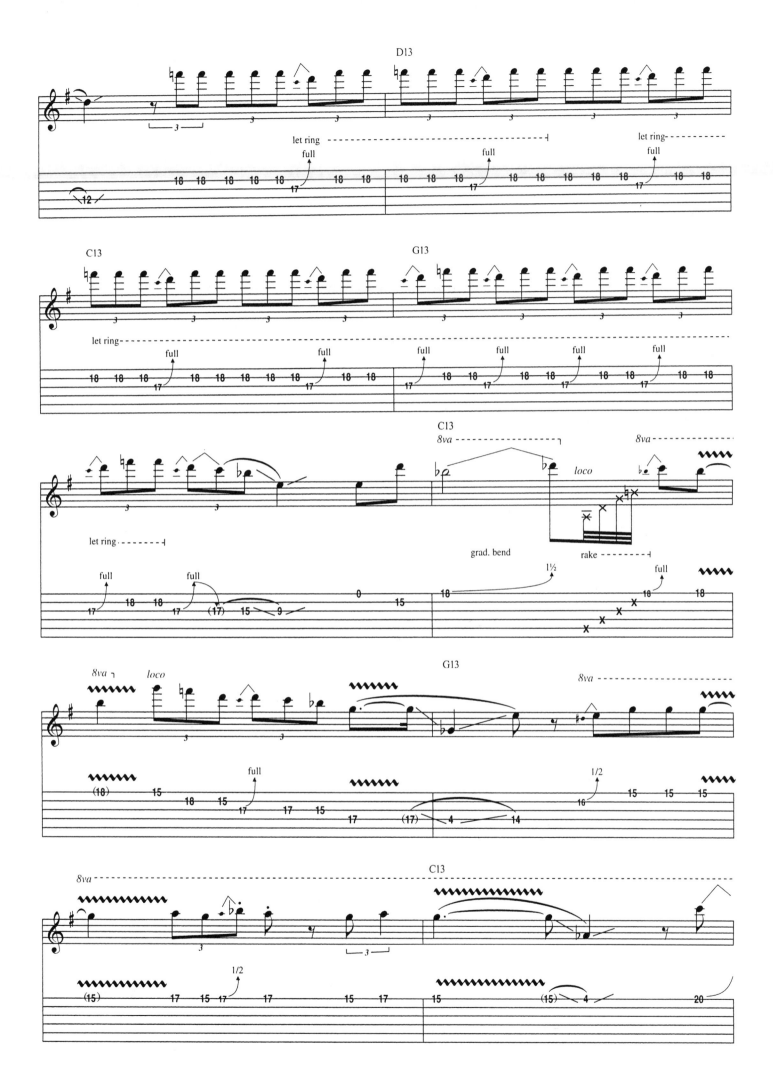

169

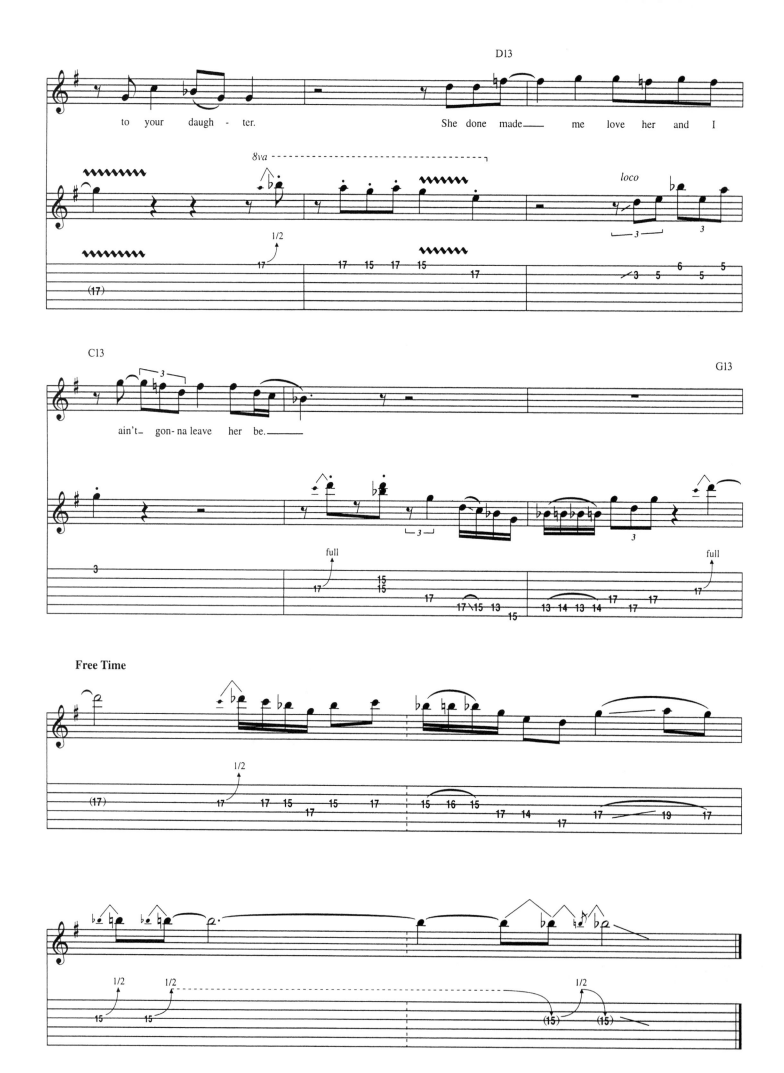

to your daugh - ter.   She done made— me love her and I

ain't— gon- na leave   her be.—

Free Time

No, No Baby

By Son Seals

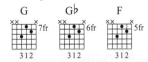

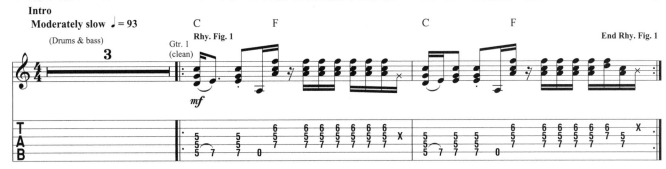

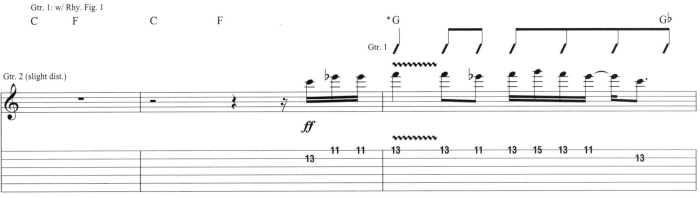

*See top of page for chord diagrams pertaining to rhythm slashes.

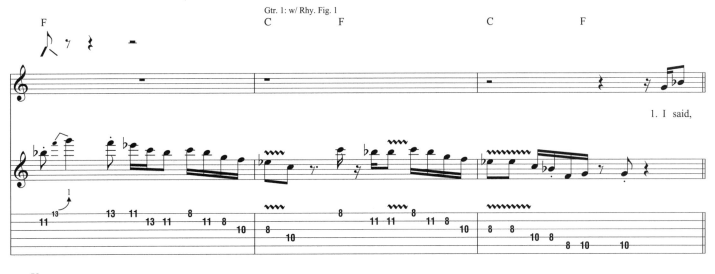

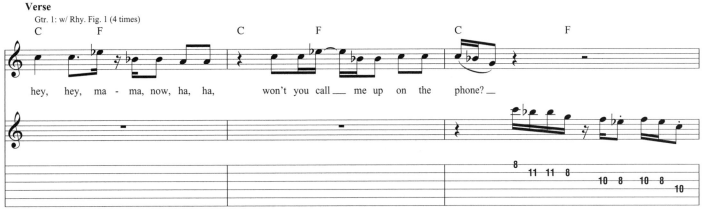

hey, hey, ma-ma, now, ha, ha, won't you call ___ me up on the phone? ___

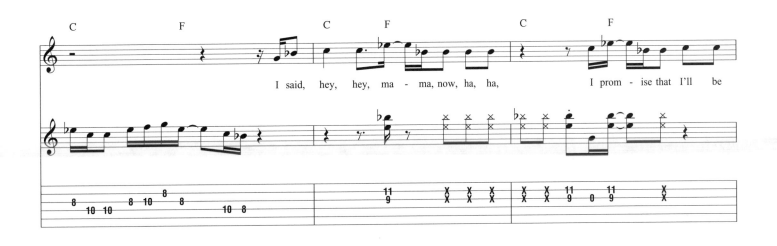

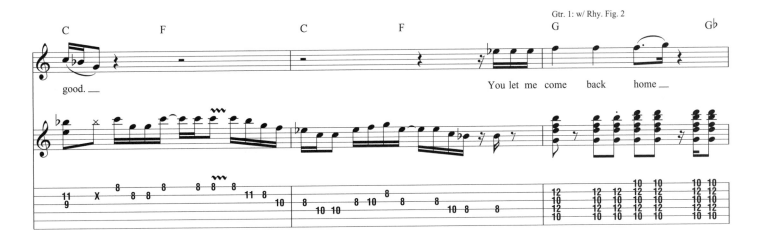

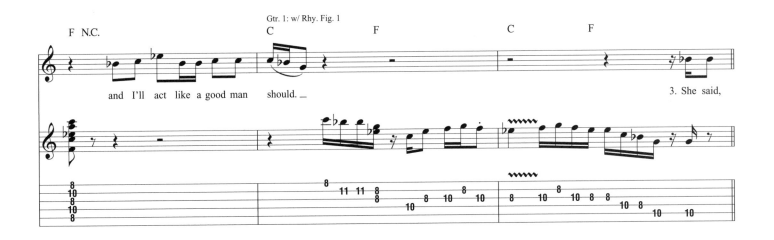

She said, "No, no, ba-by, now, ha, ha, boy,_ I'm tired_ of you do-in' me

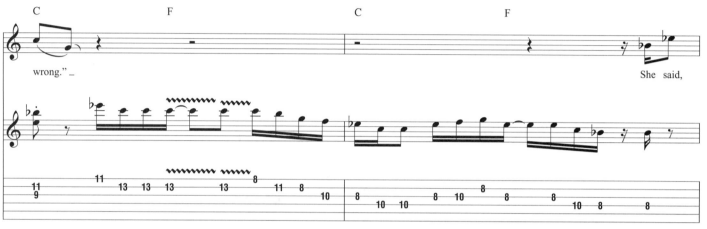

wrong."_ She said,

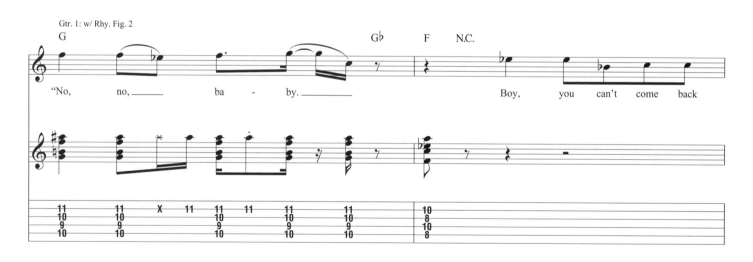

Gtr. 1: w/ Rhy. Fig. 2

"No, no,_____ ba-by._____ Boy, you can't come back

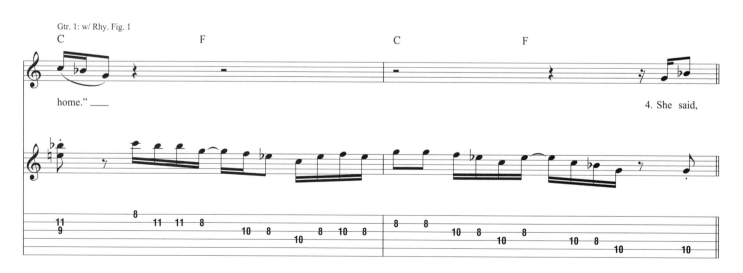

Gtr. 1: w/ Rhy. Fig. 1

home." _____ 4. She said,

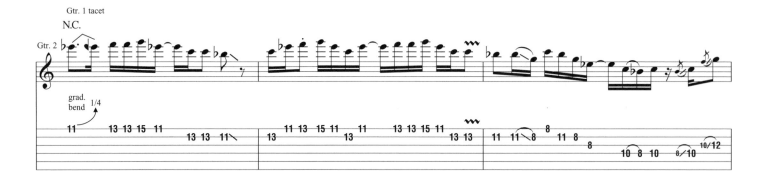

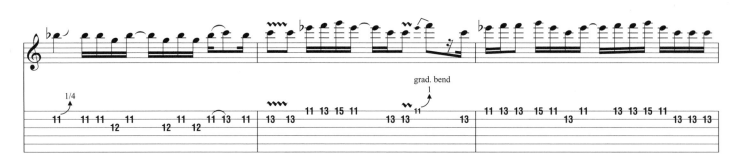

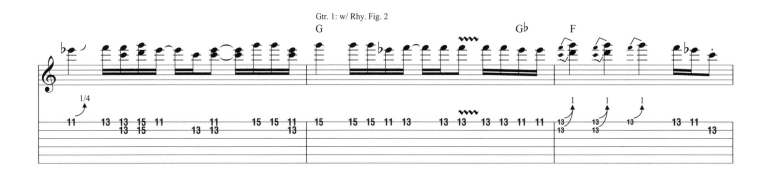

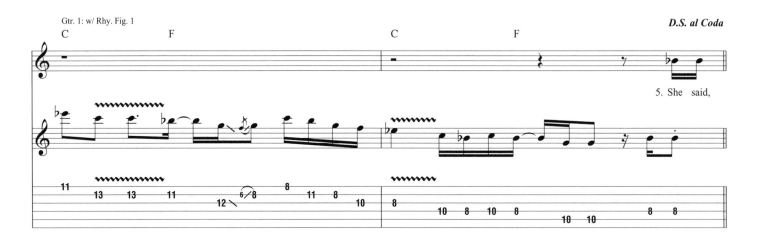

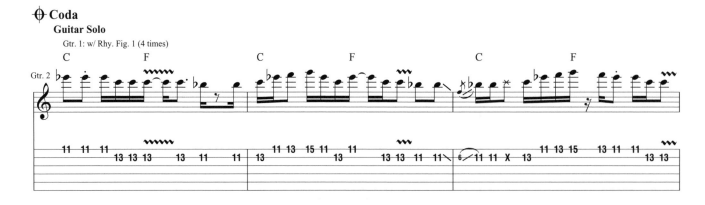

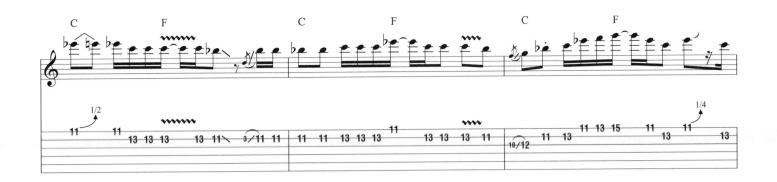

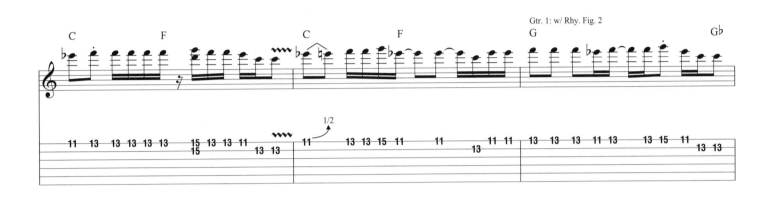

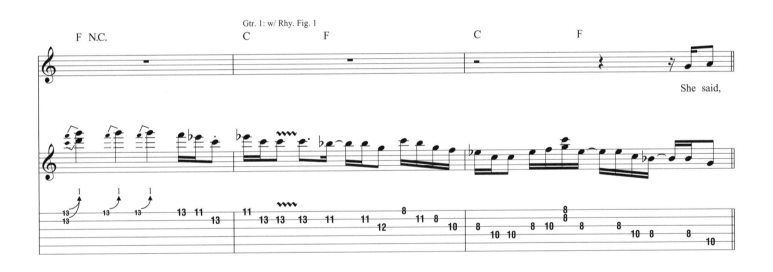

from Eric Clapton - *From the Cradle*

Reconsider Baby

Words and Music by Lowell Fulson

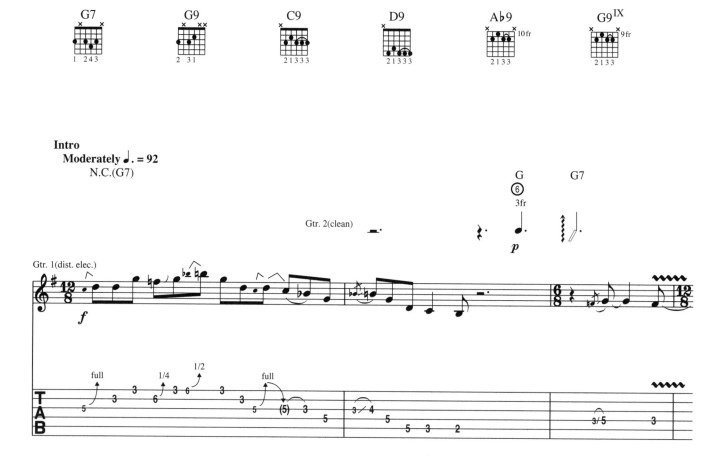

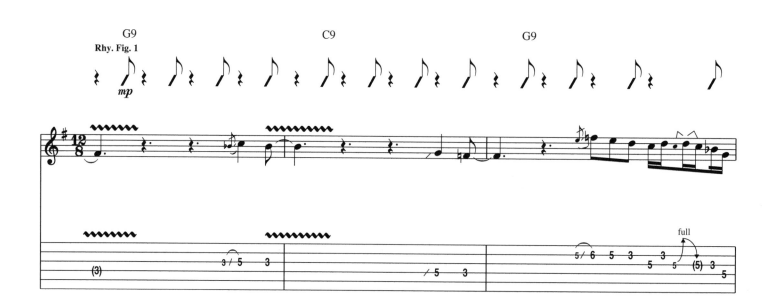

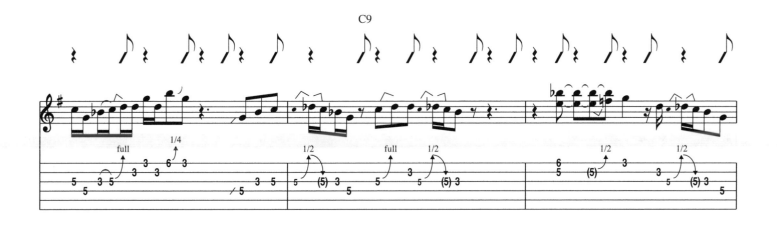

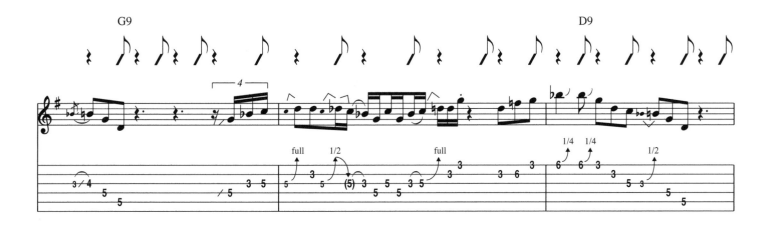

Verse

Gtr. 2: w/ Rhy. Fig. 1

___ long, _____ oh, how I hate to see you ___ go. ___

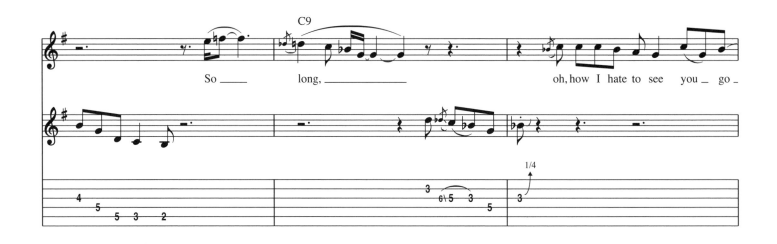

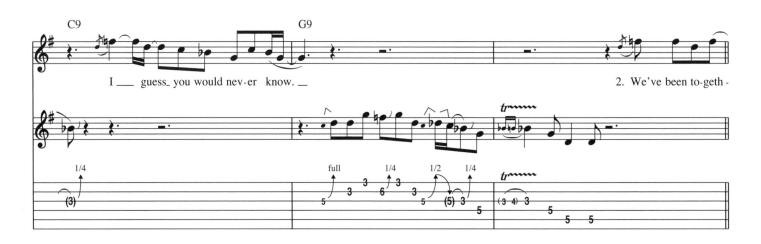

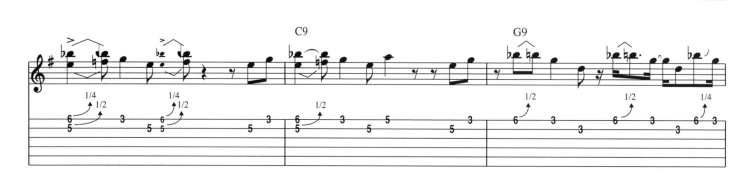
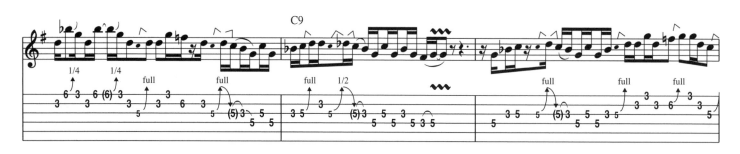
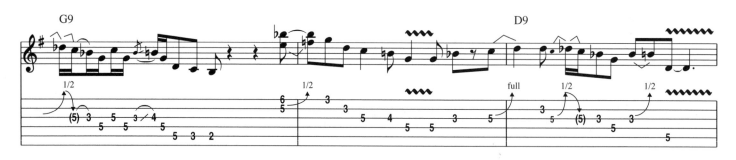
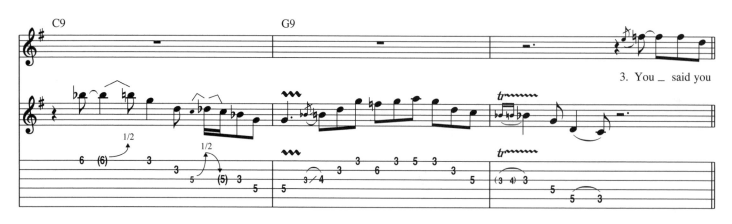

3. You __ said you

from Robert Cray - *Strong Persuader*

Right Next Door

By Dennis Walker

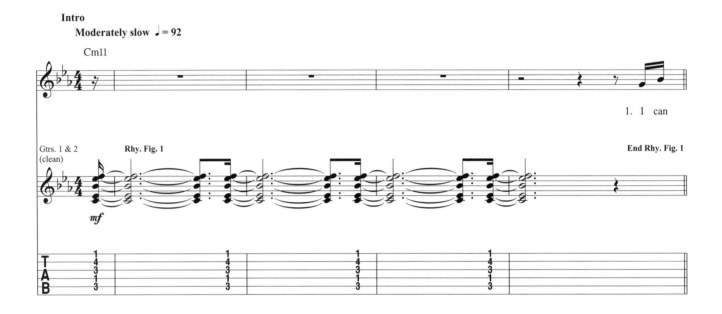

*Chord symbols reflect overall harmony.

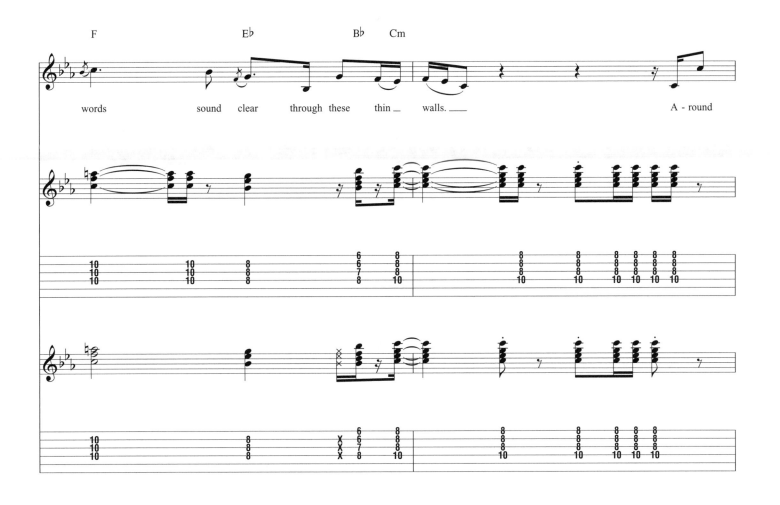

words ...... sound clear through these thin _ walls. _ A - round

mid - night I heard him shout, "Un - faith - ful wom - an," and I

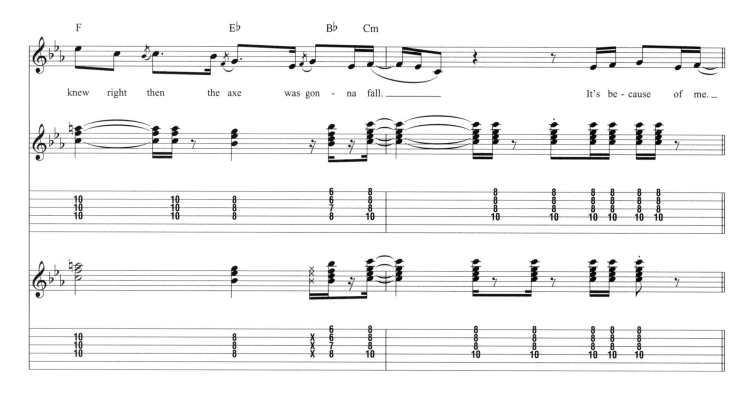

knew right then the axe was gon - na fall. _____ It's be - cause of me. _

Pre-Chorus

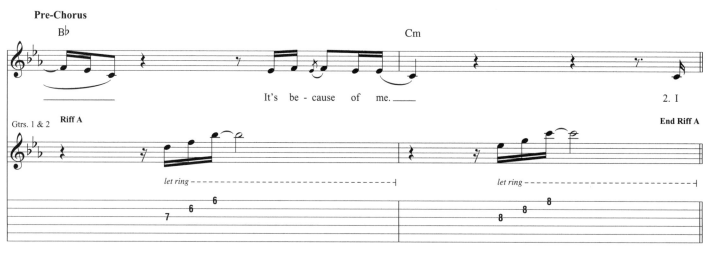

It's be - cause of me. _____ 2. I

Gtrs. 1 & 2   **Riff A**   **End Riff A**

let ring - - - - - - - - - - - - - - - - - - -   let ring - - - - - - - - - - - - - - - - - - -

Verse

heard him shout, _ "Who is ___ he?" She mum - bled low. He said,

Gtr. 1

Gtr. 2

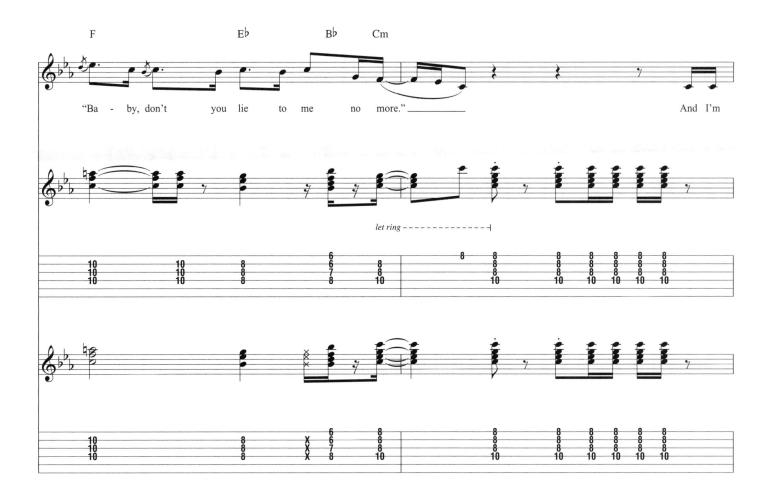

"Ba - by, don't you lie to me no more." _____ And I'm

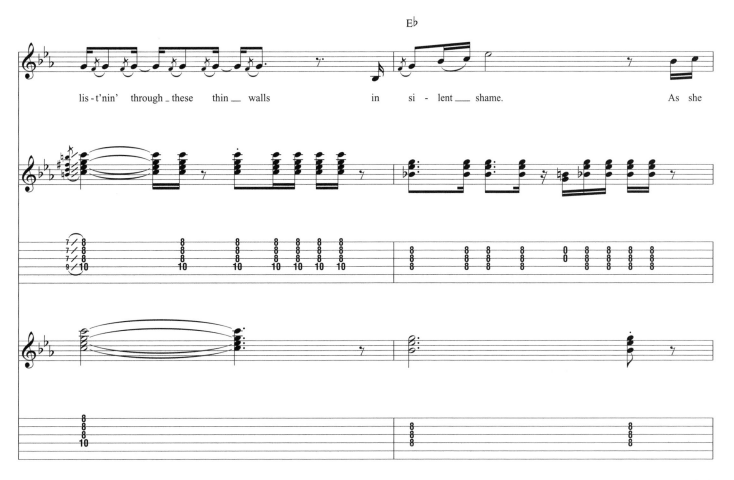

lis - t'nin' through ___ these thin ___ walls in si - lent ___ shame. As she

Pre-Chorus

Gtr. 2: w/ Riff A (2 times)

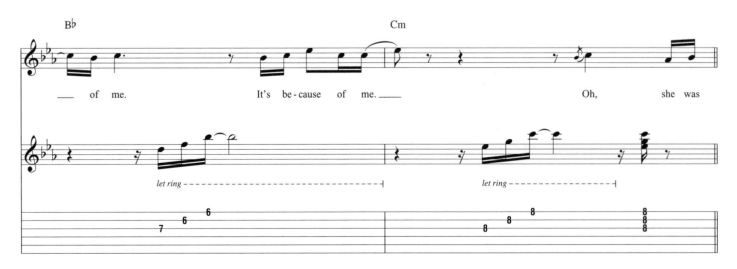

Chorus

right next door and I'm such a strong per-suad - er. _____ Well, she was

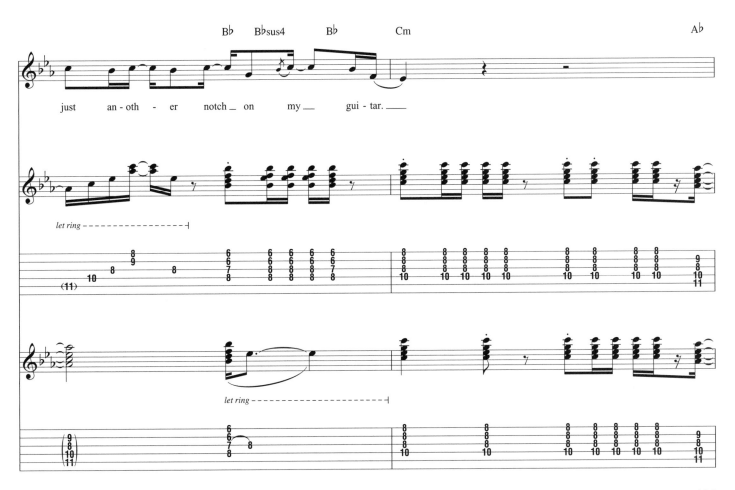

just an-oth - er notch _ on my _ gui - tar. _____

She's gon-na lose the man that real-ly loves __ her. _____ In the

si - lence I __ can hear __ their break - in' hearts. __ Oh. _____

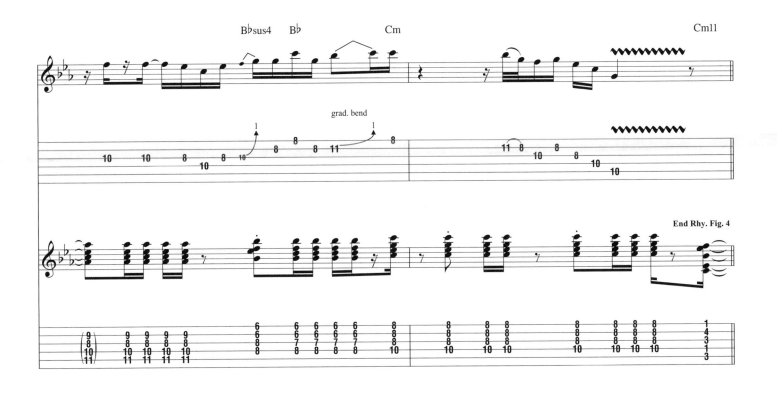

Interlude

Gtrs. 1 & 2: w/ Rhy. Fig. 1

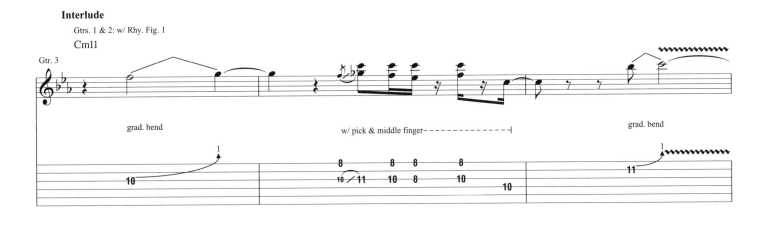

Verse

3. At day-break I hear him pack, __ say good-

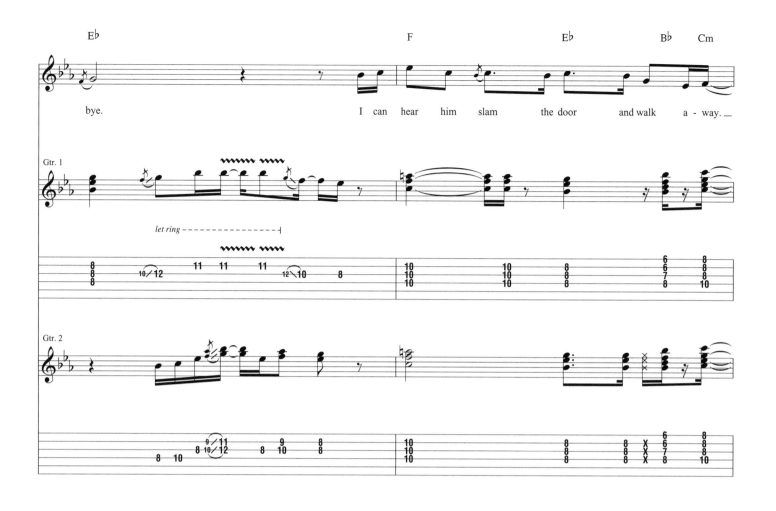

bye.   I can hear him slam the door and walk a - way.

Right next   door   I hear that wom-an   start to

*Sung behind
the beat.

196

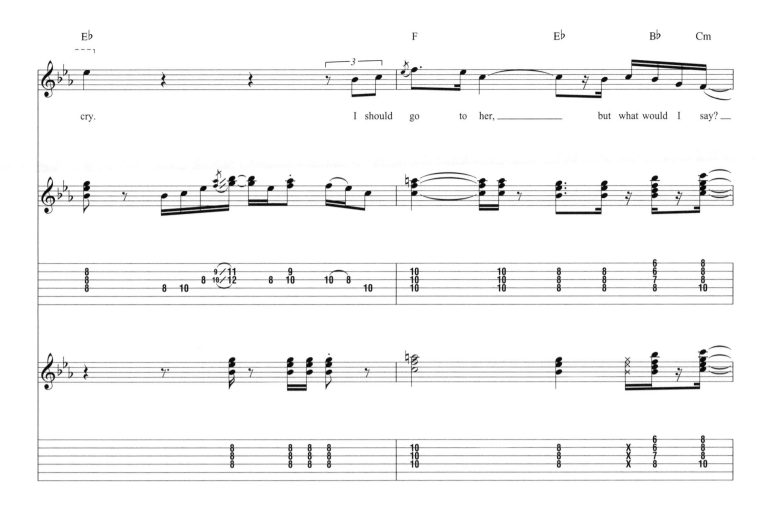

cry.   I should go to her, _____ but what would I say? ___

Pre-Chorus
Gtr. 2: w/ Riff A (2 times)

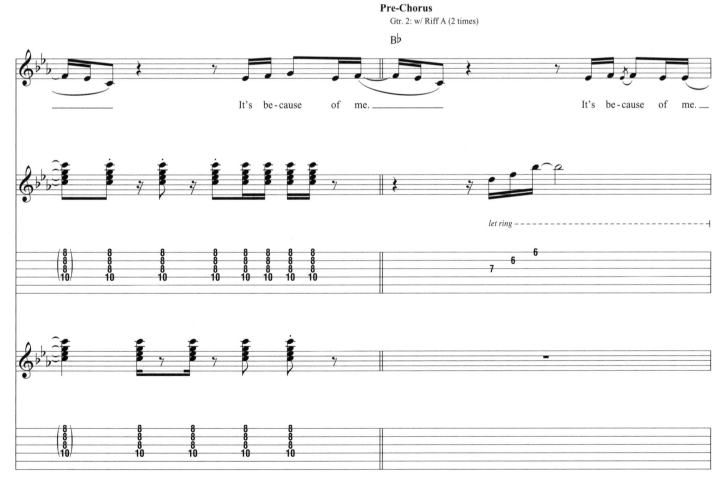

_____ It's be-cause of me. _____ It's be-cause of me. __

let ring - |

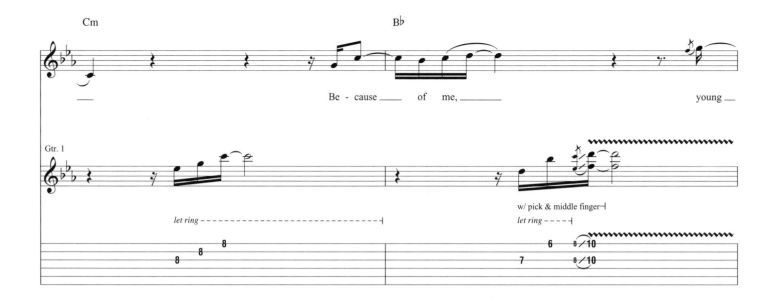

Be - cause ___ of me, ___ young ___

Chorus

___ Bob. ___ Oh, she was right next door and I'm such a strong per - suad -

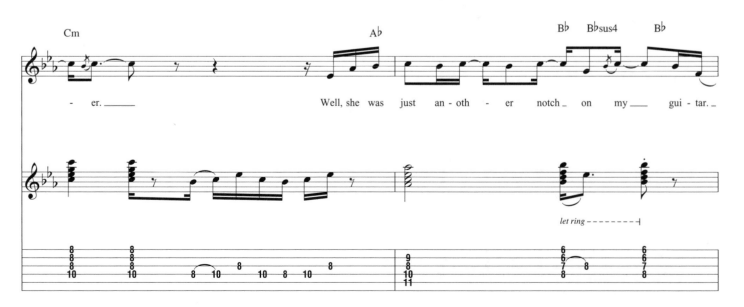

- er. ___ Well, she was just an - oth - er notch ___ on my ___ gui - tar. ___

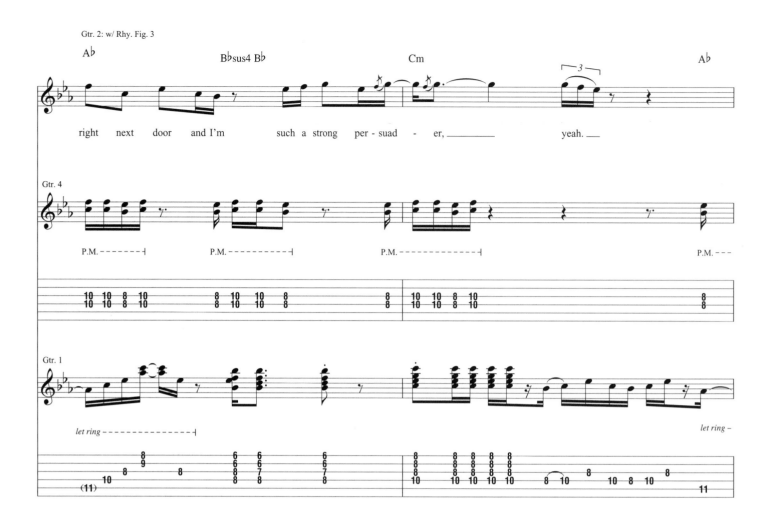

right next door and I'm such a strong per-suad-er, _____ yeah. _____

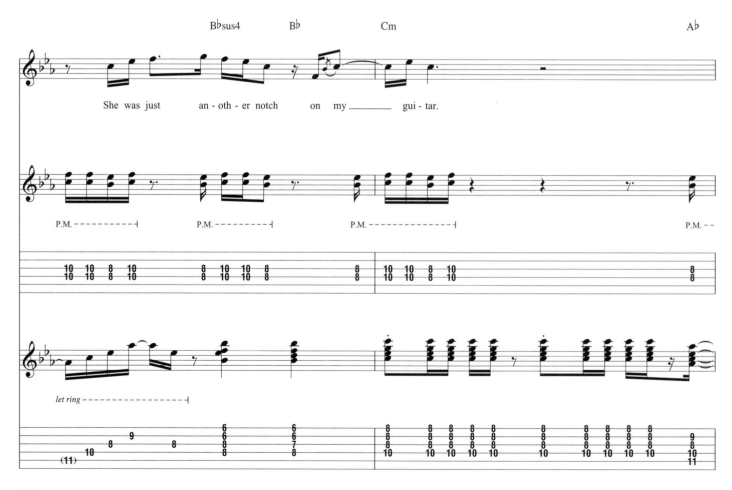

She was just an-oth-er notch on my _____ gui-tar.

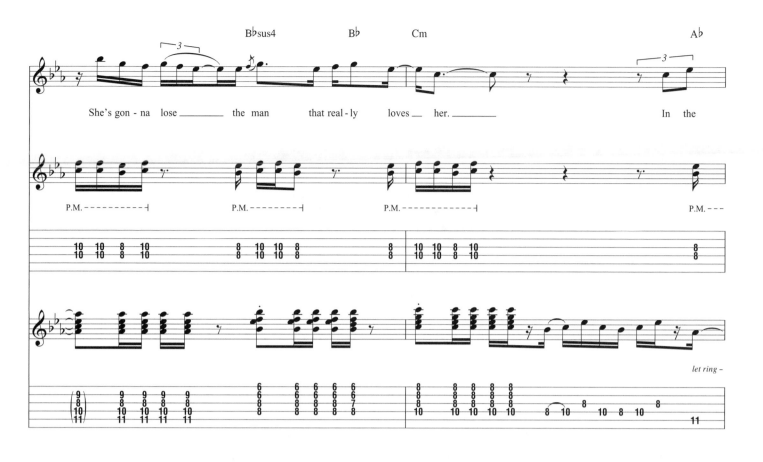

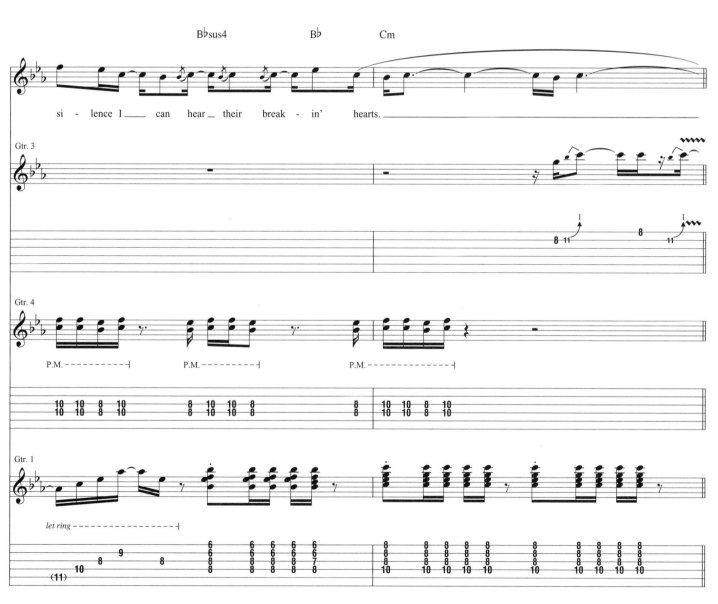

Guitar Solo

Gtrs. 1 & 2: w/ Rhy. Fig. 4
Gtr. 4 tacet

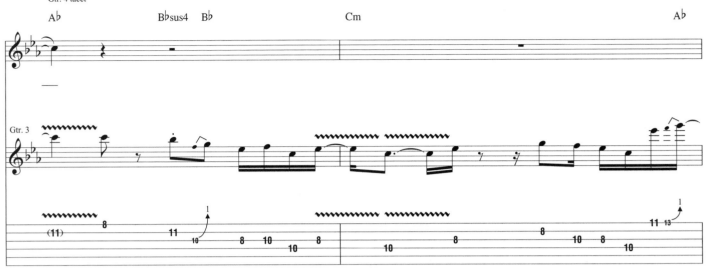

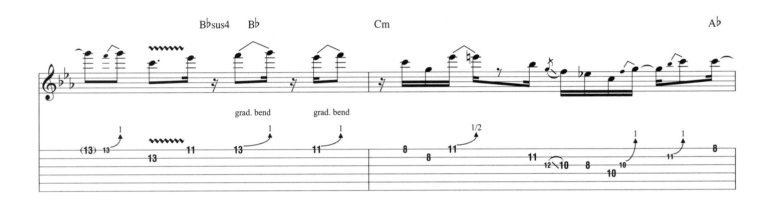

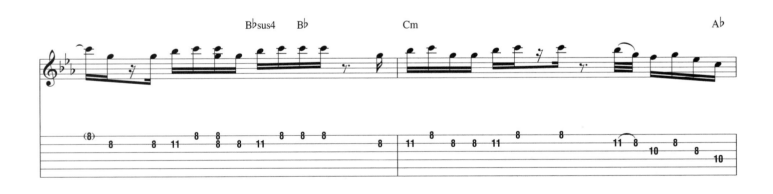

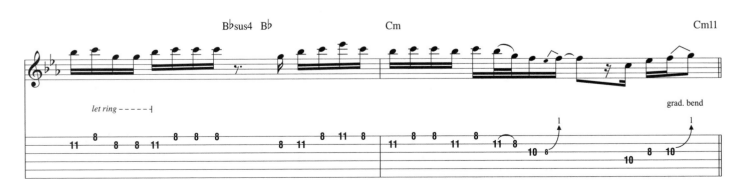

Outro

Gtrs. 1 & 2: w/ Rhy. Fig. 1 (1st 2 meas., 4 times)

Cm11

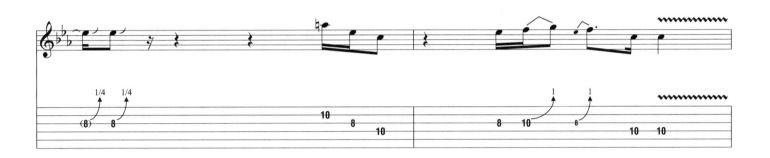

Begin fade

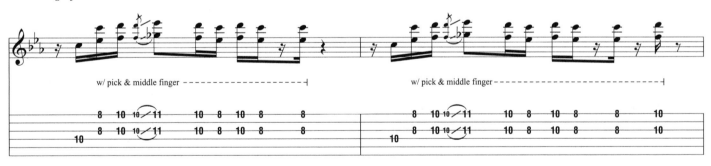

Fade out

Right Place, Wrong Time

Words and Music by Otis Rush

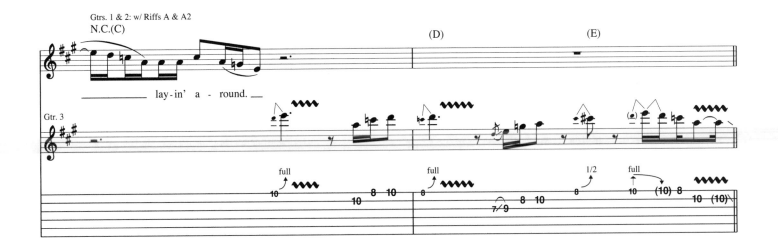

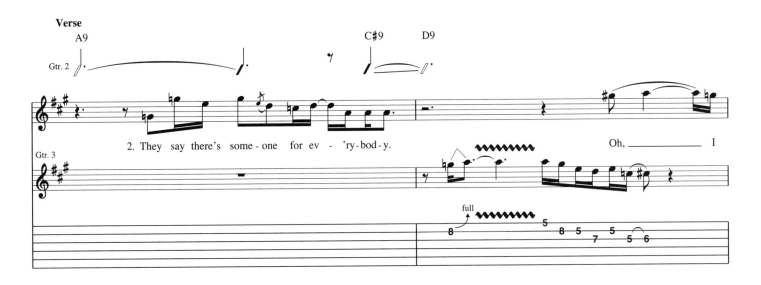

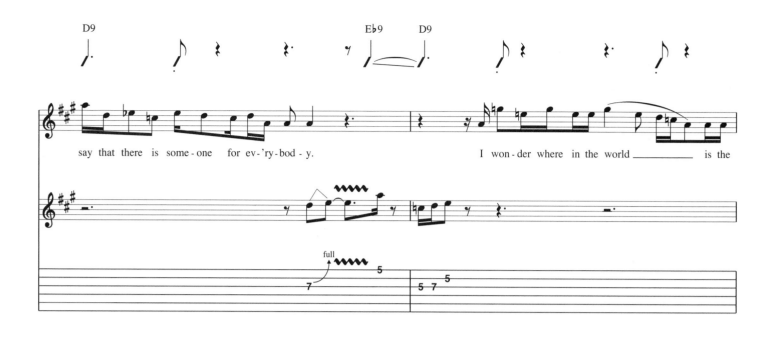

say that there is some-one for ev-'ry-bod-y.   I won-der where in the world _____ is the

one   for me. ____   An-oth-er

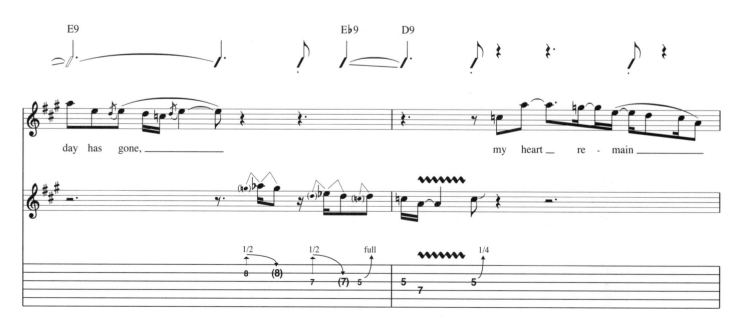

day has gone, _____   my heart __ re-main _____

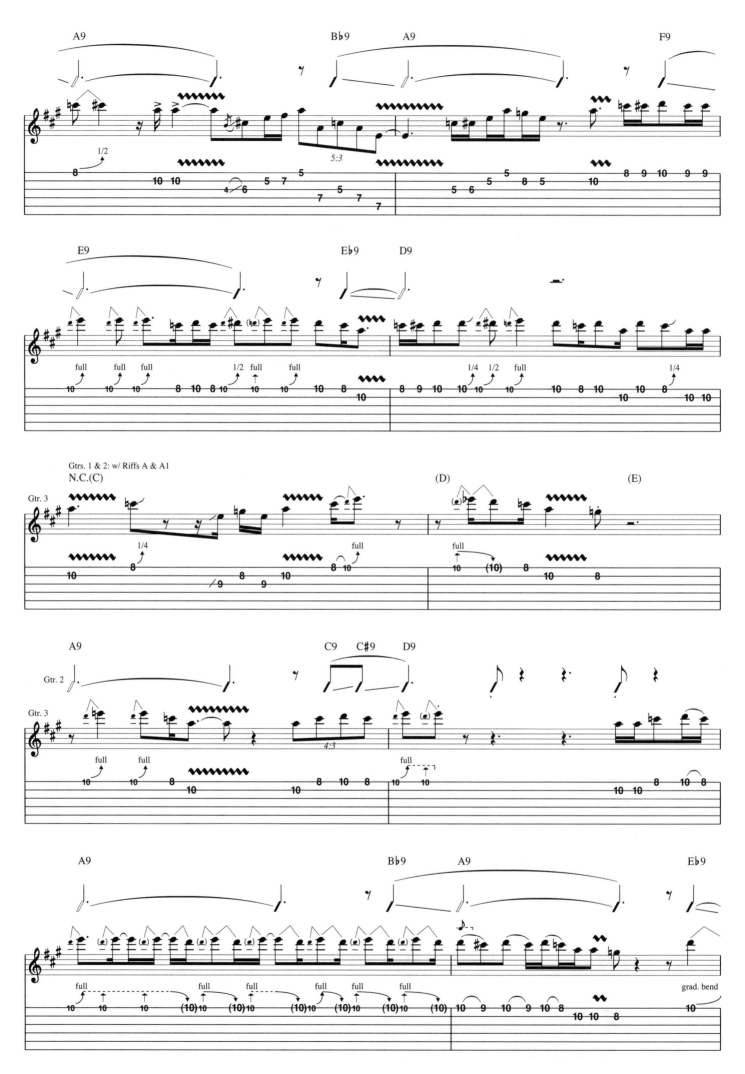

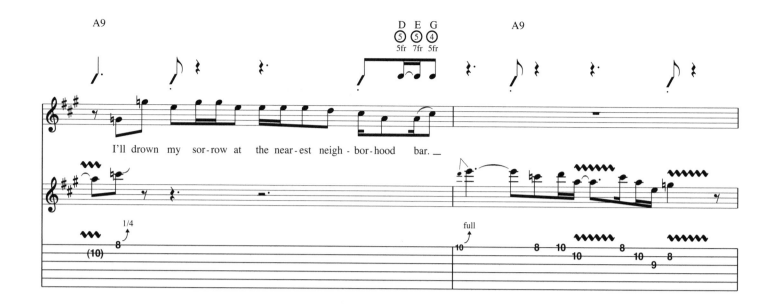

I'll drown my sor-row at the near-est neigh-bor-hood bar. —

Gtr. 2: w/ Rhy. Fill 1

Oh, _____ I think I'll go out and do the town. _____ I'll drown _

my sor-row at the near-est neigh-bor-hood bar. _ I think I'll

Rhy. Fill 1
Gtr. 2

(cont. in slash)

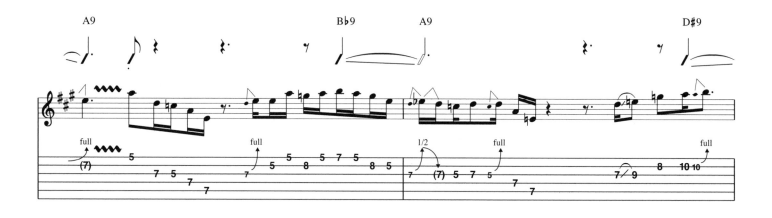

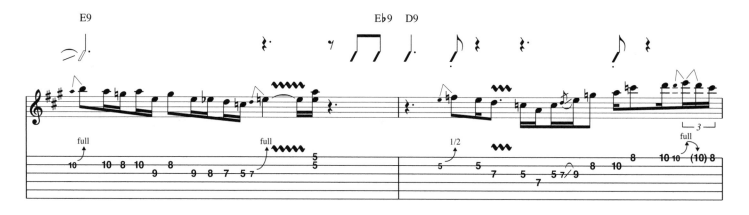

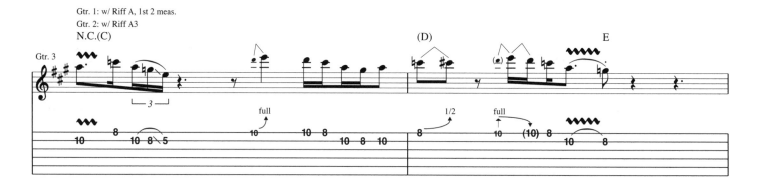

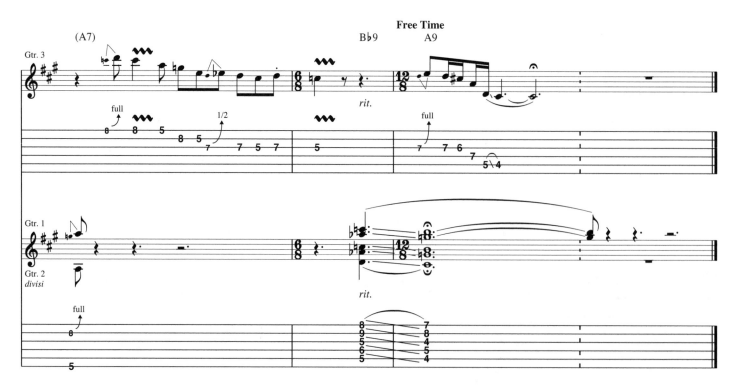

from Lonnie Mack - *Strike Like Lightning*

Satisfy Susie

Words and Music by Lonnie McIntosh and Tim Drummond

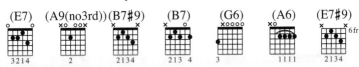

(E7) (A9(no3rd)) (B7#9) (B7) (G6) (A6) (E7#9)

† Gtrs. 1 & 2;
Tune Down 1 Step, Capo III:

① = D   ④ = C
② = A   ⑤ = G
③ = F   ⑥ = D

Gtr. 3; Tune Down 1/2 Step:

① = Eb   ④ = Db
② = Bb   ⑤ = Ab
③ = Gb   ⑥ = Eb

Intro
Moderately ♩ = 135

N.C.

* (E7)

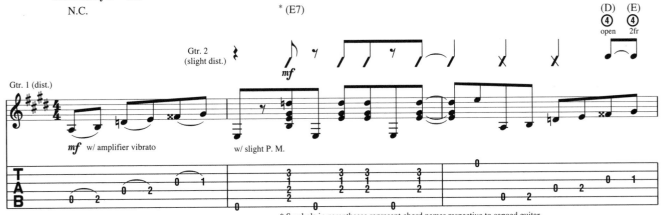

* Symbols in parentheses represent chord names respective to capoed guitar
and do not reflect actual sounding chords. Capoed fret is "0" in TAB.

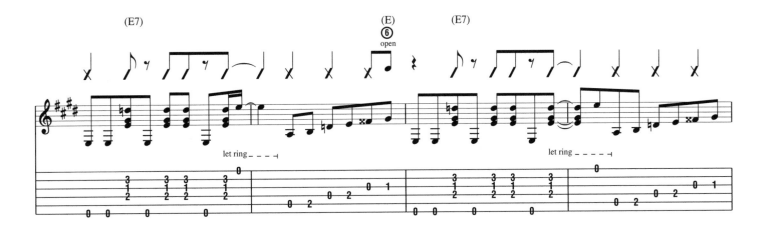

† Editor's note: You can accomplish the same result without tuning down a whole step by remaining in standard tuning and capoing at the first fret.

Copyright © 1985 Mack's Flying V Music (BMI) and Dragon River Music (BMI)
All Rights for Mack's Flying V Music Administered by Conexion Entertainment Group
All Rights for Dragon River Music Administered by MCS America, Inc.
International Copyright Secured All Rights Reserved Used by Permission

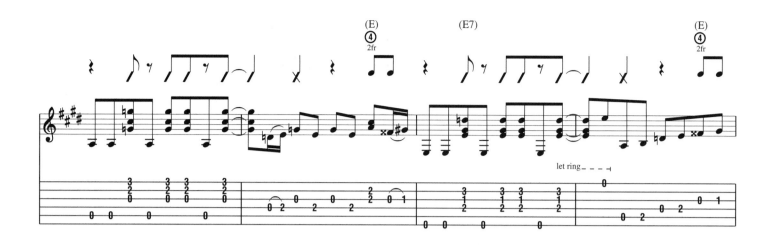

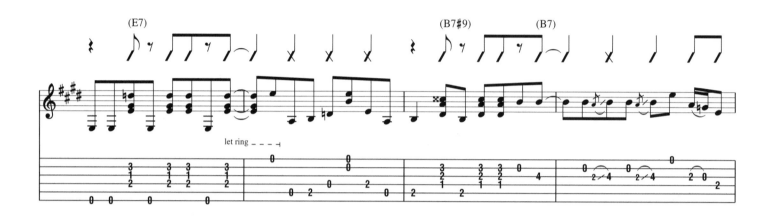

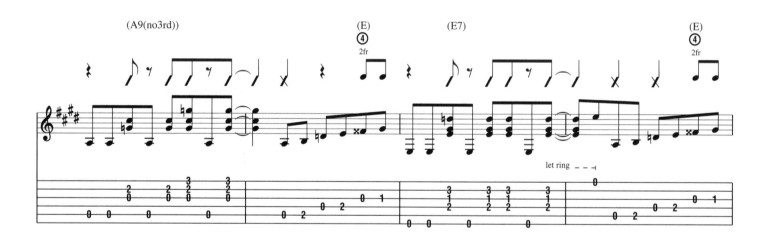

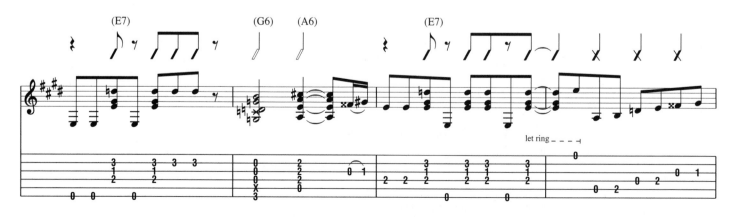

Verse

1. Can I tell ya 'bout my ba - by, she's
2., 3., 4. *See Additional Lyrics*

Riff A

let ring _ _ _ _ _ _

ev - 'ry man's dream? She could be the fold - out in a gir - ly ma - ga - zine. I got to

End Riff A

Chorus

sat - is - fy Su - sie.
(You got to sat - is - fy Su - sie.

I got to sa - tis - fy Su - sie.

Riff B

I got to sat-is-fy Su-sie, Su-sie sure sat-is-fies

(Sa-tis-fy Su-sie.)

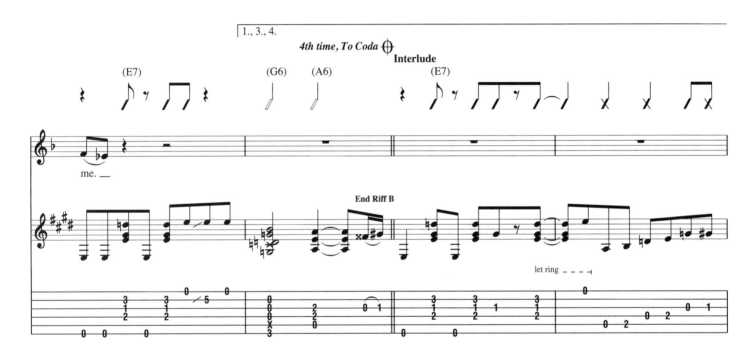

me.

Interlude

End Riff B

let ring

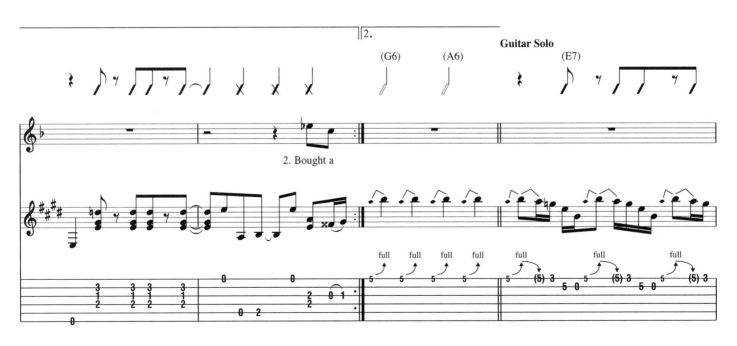

2. Bought a

Guitar Solo

full full full full full full full

218

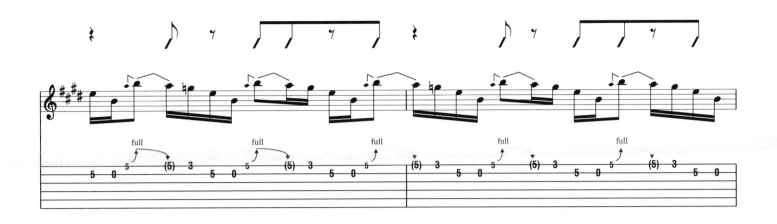

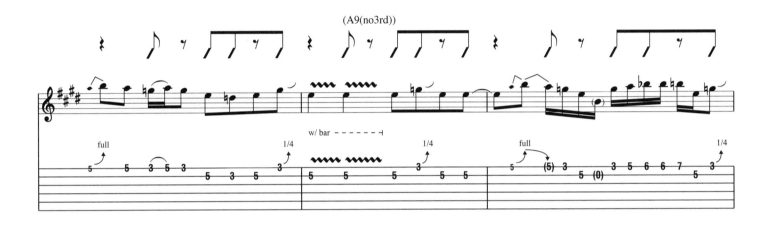

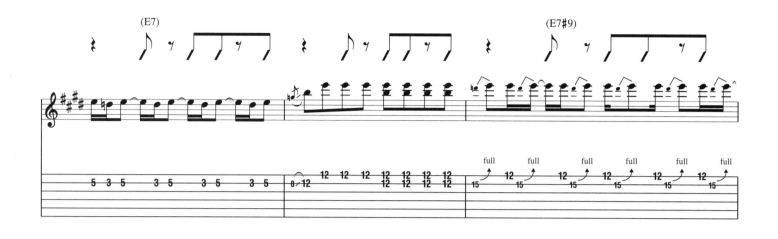

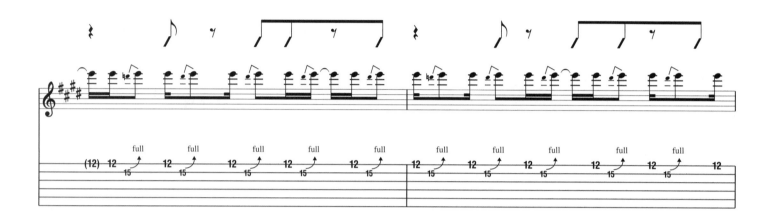

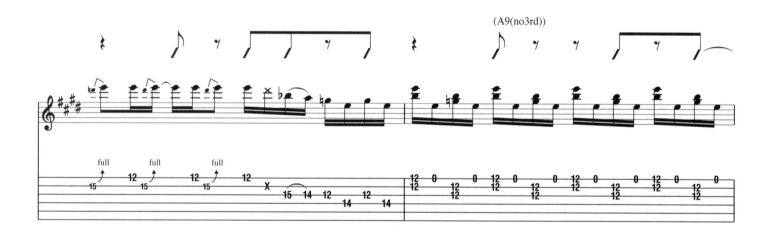

* Stevie Ray Vaughan

Guitar Solo

Gtr. 1: w/ Riff A, simile
Gtr. 2 tacet

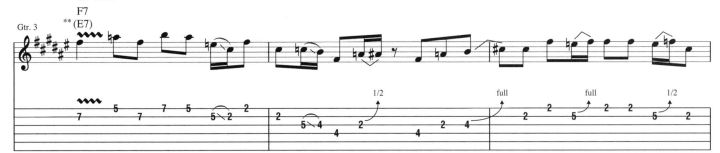

** Symbols in parentheses represent chord names respective to capoed guitar.
 Symbols above reflect actual sounding chords. Chord symbols reflect implied harmony.

Gtr. 1: w/ Riff B, 1st 6 meas., simile

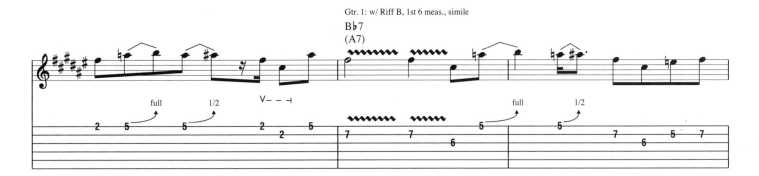

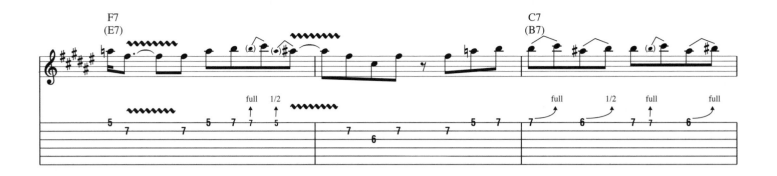

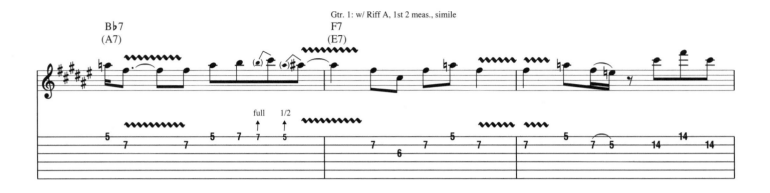

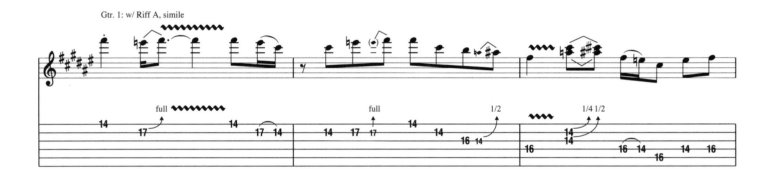

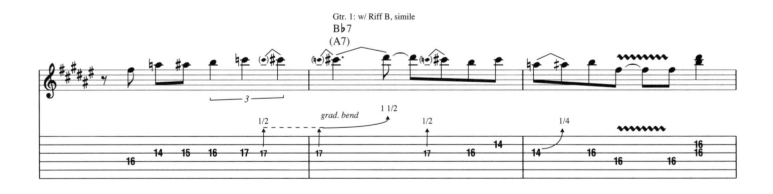

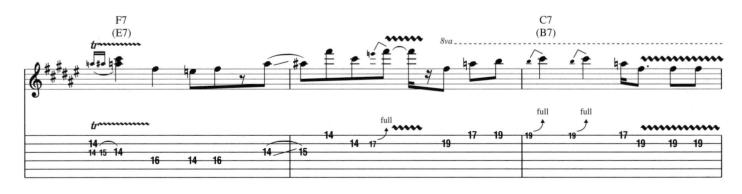

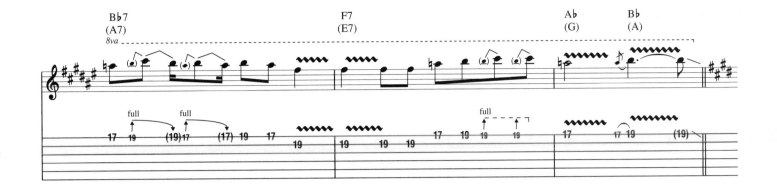

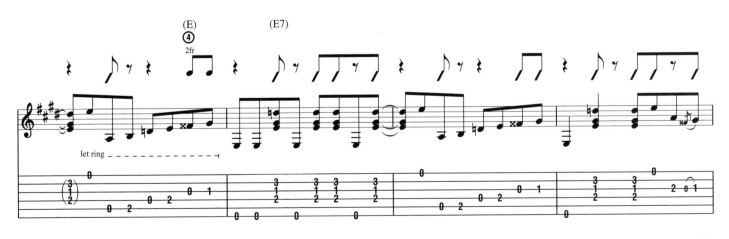

Outro

Got - ta sat - is - fy Su - sie, Su - sie sure sa - tis - fies ___

me. ___

Additional Lyrics

2. Bought a brand new Chevy,
   Keep it shined up in the drive.
   Souped up to the limit
   'Cause Susie likes to fly it.

3. Susie's into lovin'
   Anyway you can.
   She don't give her lovin'
   To any other man.

4. You ask me if I'm happy,
   Do I look satisfied?
   Susie's got the way to keep
   The twinkle in my eye.

Shelter Me

Words and Music by Julie Miller and Buddy Miller

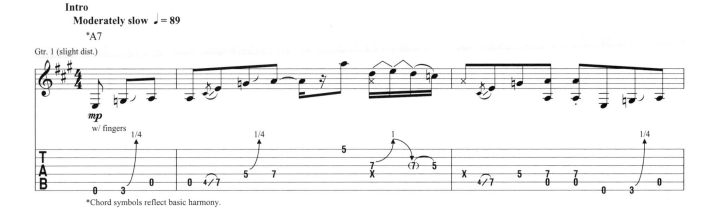

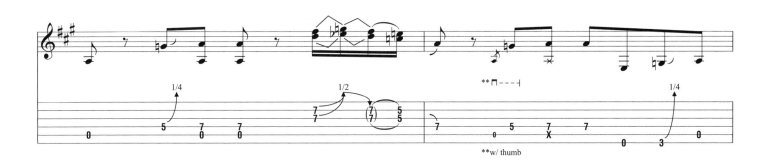

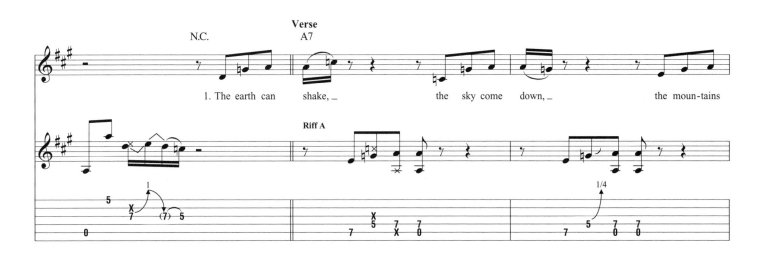

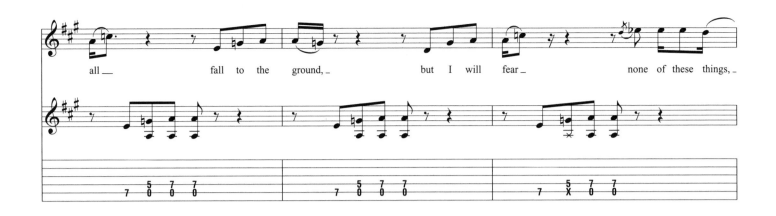

all ___ fall to the ground, ___ but I will fear ___ none of these things, ___

G5 E5 D5 C5 A7   N.C.

___ a, shel-ter me, Lord, ___ un-der-neath your ___ wings.   2. Dark wa-ters

Verse
Gtr. 1: w/ Riff A (1st 6 meas.)
A7

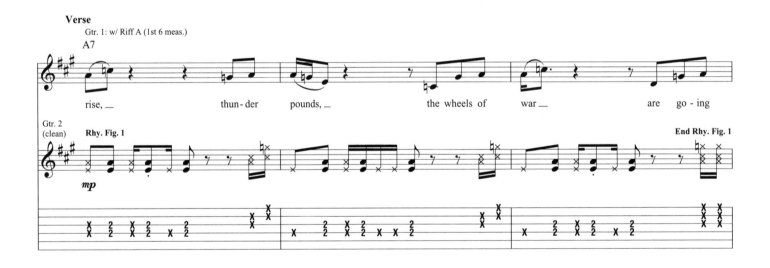

rise, ___ thun-der pounds, ___ the wheels of war ___ are go-ing

Gtr. 2 (clean) **Rhy. Fig. 1**   **End Rhy. Fig. 1**

mp

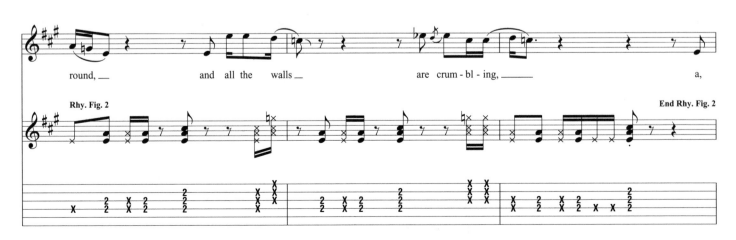

round, ___ and all the walls ___ are crum-bl-ing, _____ a,

Rhy. Fig. 2   **End Rhy. Fig. 2**

shel - ter me, Lord, __ un - der - neath your __ wing, __ shel - ter me, Lord, __ un - der -

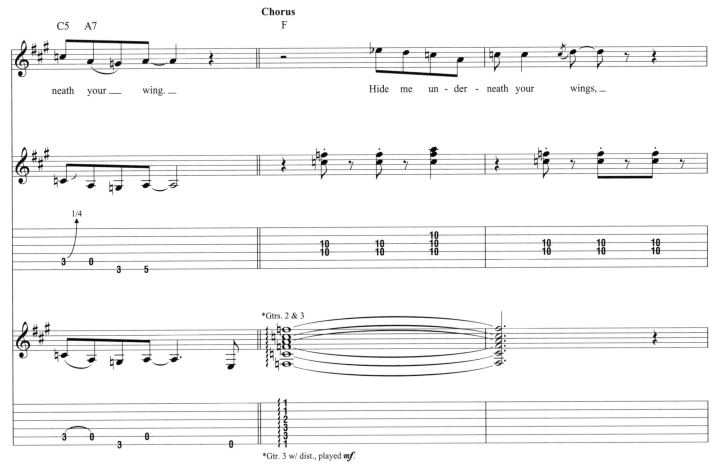

neath your __ wing. __ Hide me un - der - neath your wings, __

*Gtr. 3 w/ dist., played *mf*.

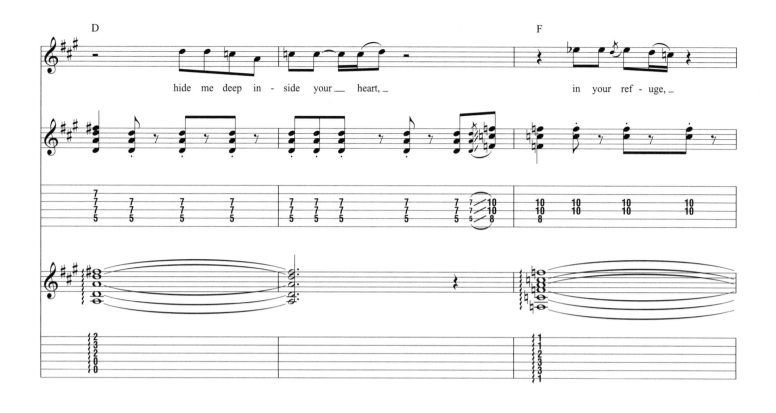

hide me deep in - side your ___ heart, ___ in your ref - uge, ___

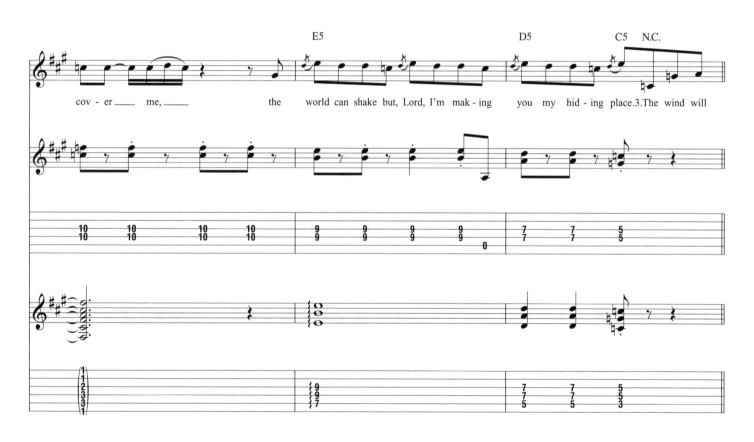

cov - er ___ me, ___ the world can shake but, Lord, I'm mak - ing you my hid - ing place. 3. The wind will

Verse

Gtr. 1: w/ Riff A (1st 6 meas.)
Gtr. 2: w/ Rhy. Fig. 1
Gtr. 3 tacet

blow, the rain can pour, ___ the del - uge breaks, ___ the tem - pest

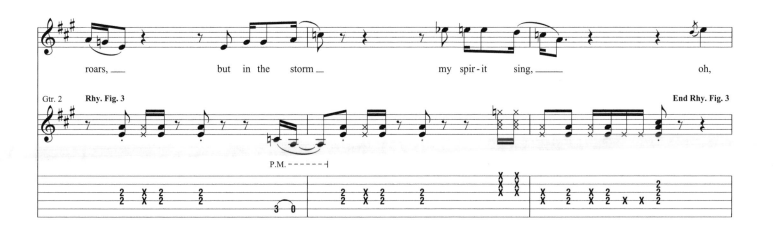

roars, ___ but in the storm ___ my spir-it sing, ___ oh,

Gtr. 2 **Rhy. Fig. 3**   **End Rhy. Fig. 3**

P.M. - - - - - - ┤

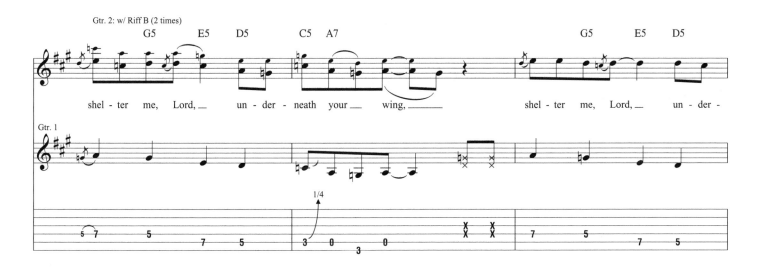

Gtr. 2: w/ Riff B (2 times)

G5   E5   D5   C5   A7   G5   E5   D5

shel - ter me, Lord, ___ un - der - neath your ___ wing, ___ shel - ter me, Lord, ___ un - der -

Gtr. 1

1/4

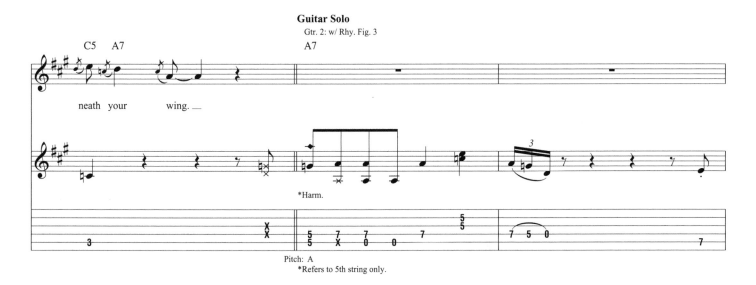

Guitar Solo
Gtr. 2: w/ Rhy. Fig. 3

C5   A7   A7

neath your   wing. ___

*Harm.

Pitch: A
*Refers to 5th string only.

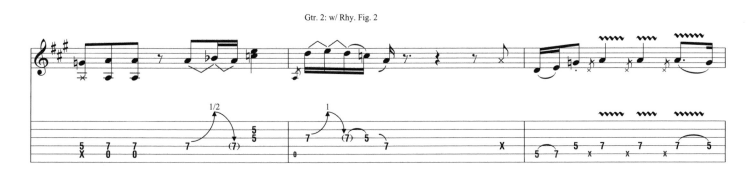

Gtr. 2: w/ Rhy. Fig. 2

1/2   1

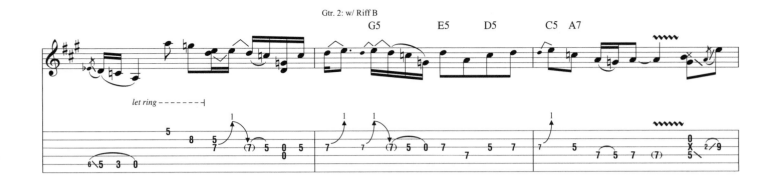

G5   E5   D5   C5   A7

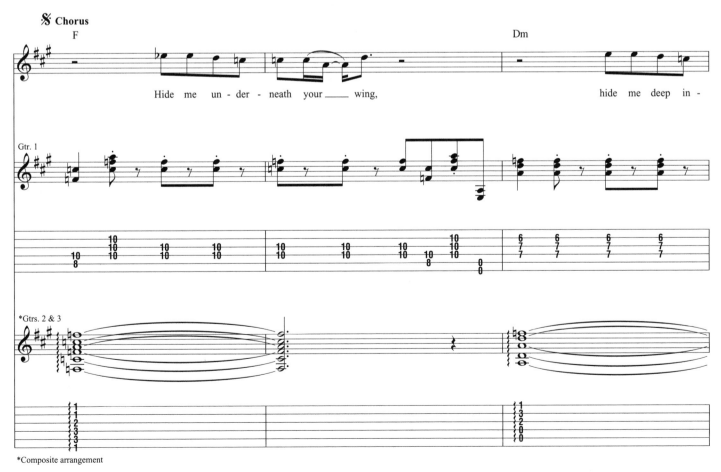

𝄋 **Chorus**

F   Dm

Hide me un-der-neath your ___ wing,   hide me deep in -

Gtr. 1

*Gtrs. 2 & 3

*Composite arrangement

⊕ Coda

Verse

Gtrs. 1 & 3 tacet
Gtr. 2: w/ Rhy. Fig.1

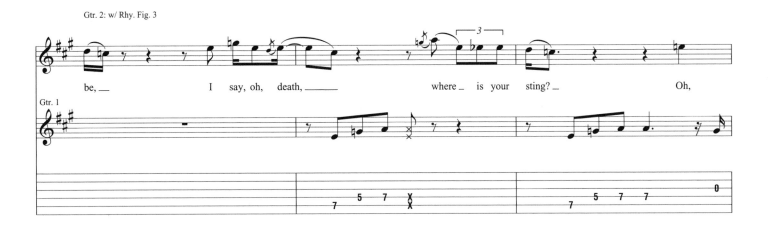

___ you call for me, some-day when time ___ no more shall

Gtr. 2: w/ Rhy. Fig. 3

be, ___ I say, oh, death, ___ where ___ is your sting? ___ Oh,

Gtr. 1

Gtr. 2: w/ Riff B (1 1/2 times)

shel-ter me, Lord, ___ un-der-neath your ___ wings, ___ I say, shel-ter me, Lord, ___ un-der-

neath your ___ wing, ___ shel-ter me, Lord, ___ un-der-neath your ___ wings. ___

Gtr. 1

Gtr. 2

Still Rainin'

Words and Music by Bruce McCabe

Verse

Gtr. 3 tacet   Gtr. 1 tacet

1. Clouds, ___ one by one, ___ fill the sky, _____ just like these tears that

Gtr. 2

let ring - - - -

Gtr. 1

End Rhy. Fig. 1

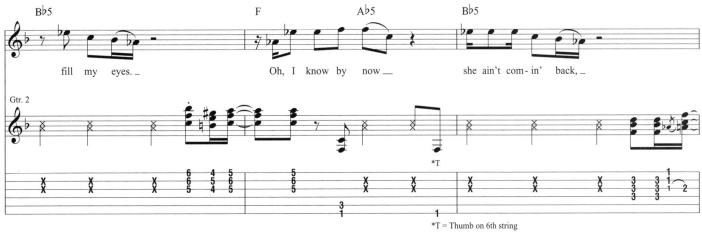

fill my eyes. ___ Oh, I know by now ___ she ain't com-in' back, ___

Gtr. 2

*T

*T = Thumb on 6th string

237

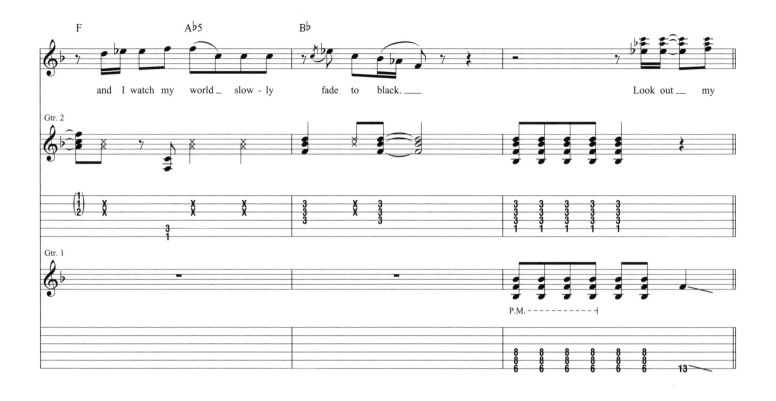

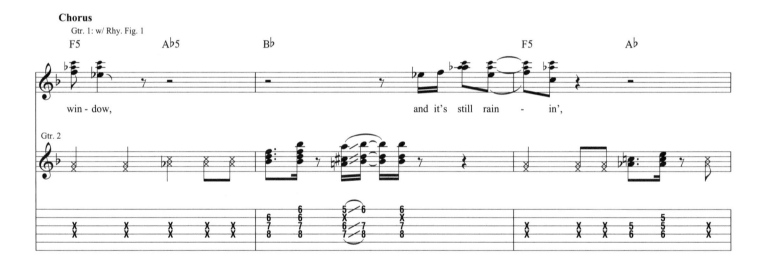

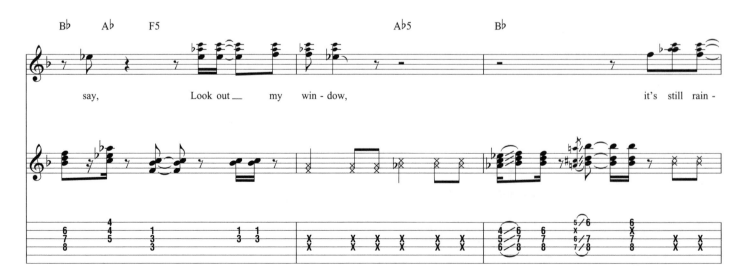

-in'. 2. Well, they say that time,— huh,

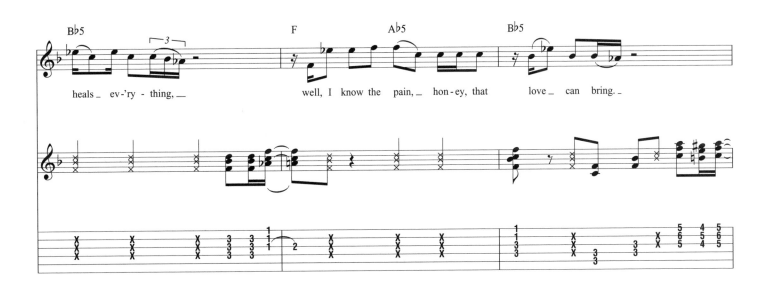

heals — ev-'ry-thing, — well, I know the pain, — hon-ey, that love — can bring. —

It don't get no bet-ter with each pass-ing day, — and ev-'ry hope I had's — slow-ly

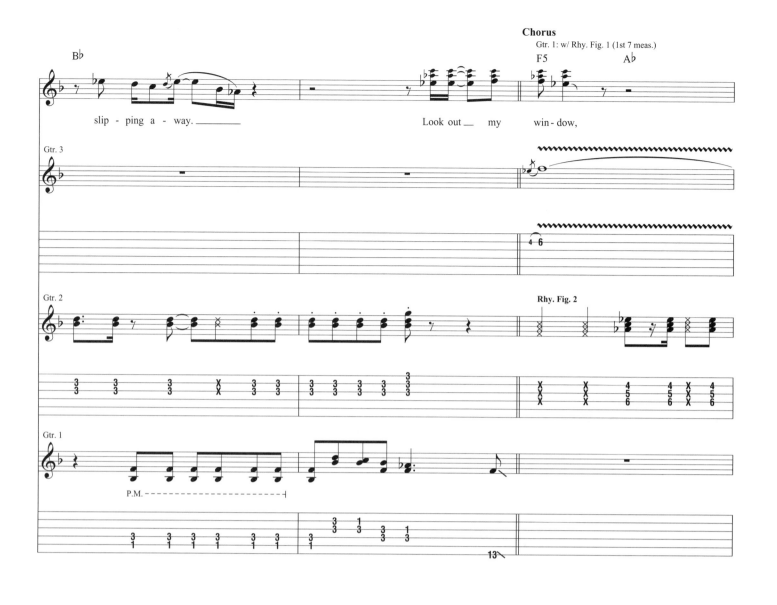

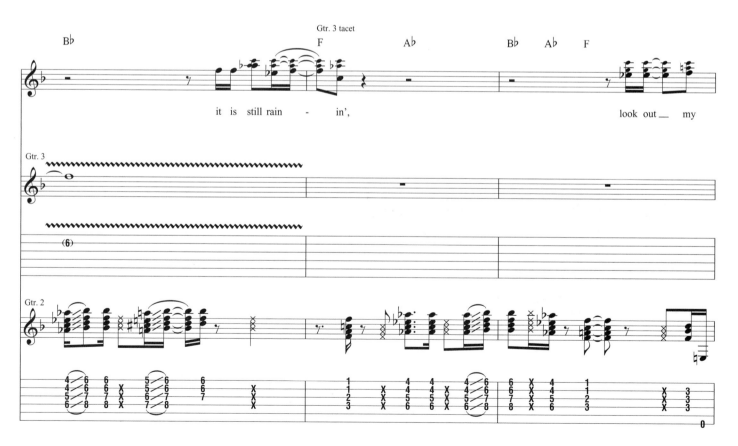

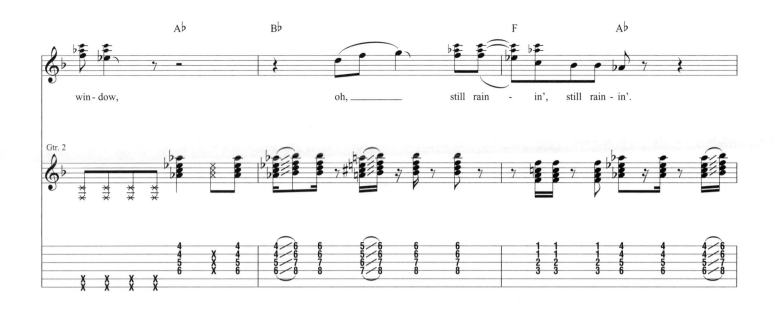

win - dow,   oh, _____ still rain - in', still rain - in'.

Bridge

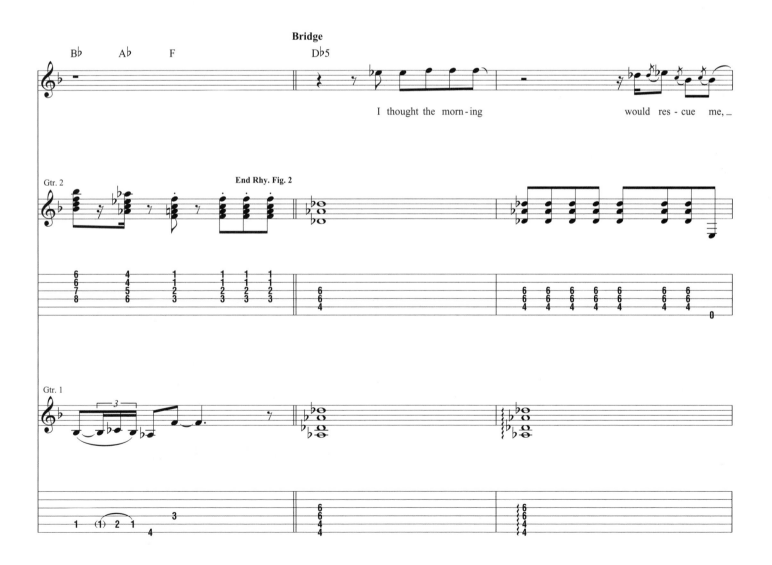

I thought the morn-ing   would res - cue me, _

End Rhy. Fig. 2

Guitar Solo

Gtr. 1: w/ Rhy. Fig. 1 (1st 4 meas., 2 times)
Gtr. 2: w/ Rhy. Fig. 2

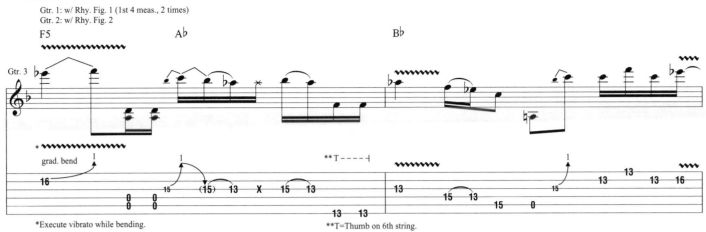

*Execute vibrato while bending.   **T=Thumb on 6th string.

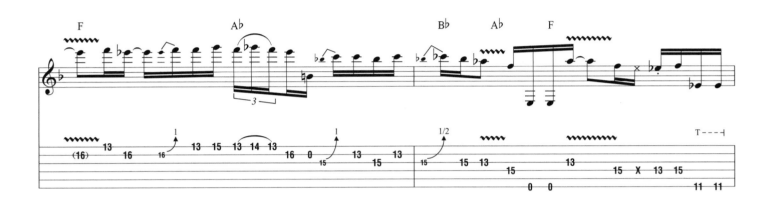

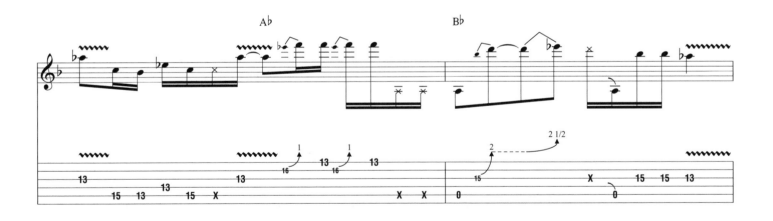

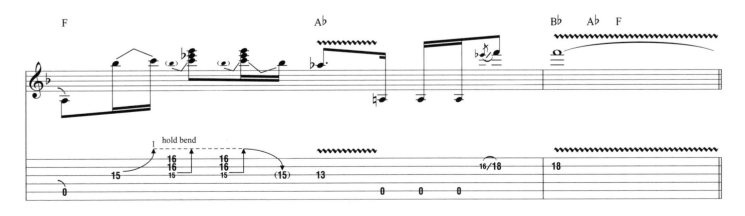

Interlude

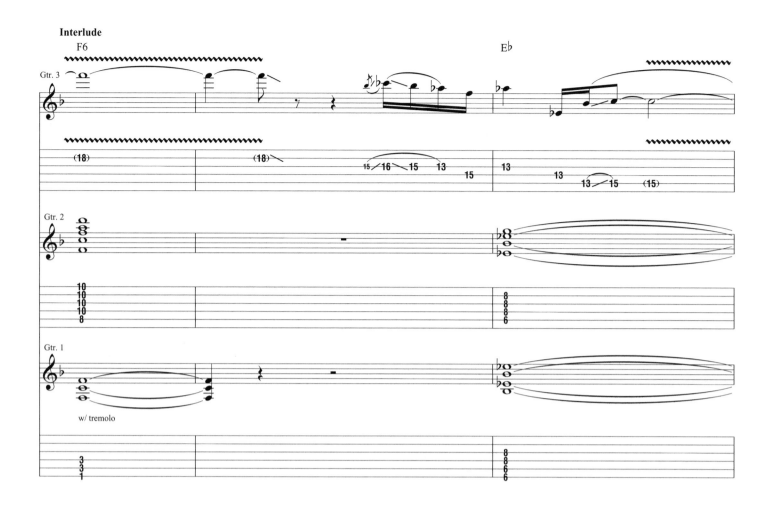

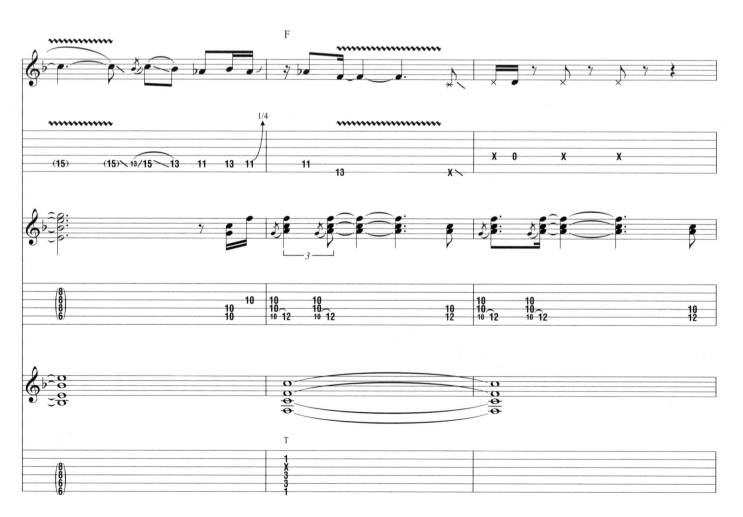

Verse

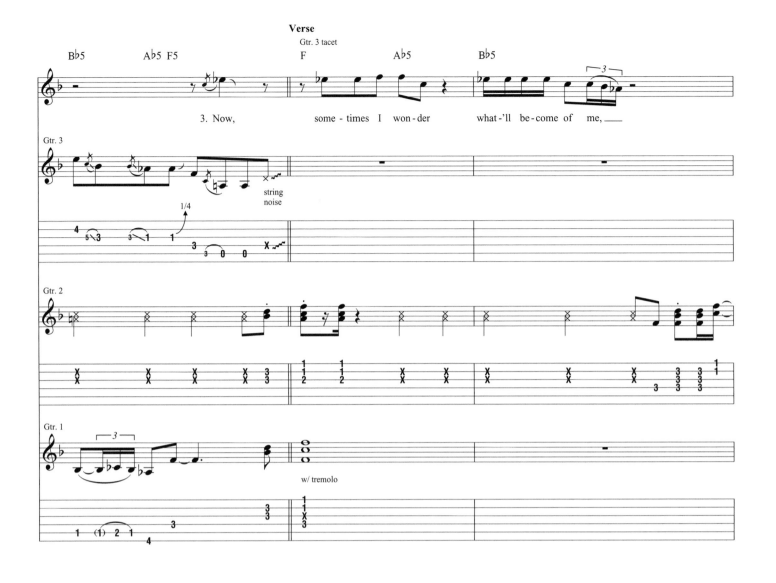

there ain't much left of what I ____ used to be.   Her love shone on me   just

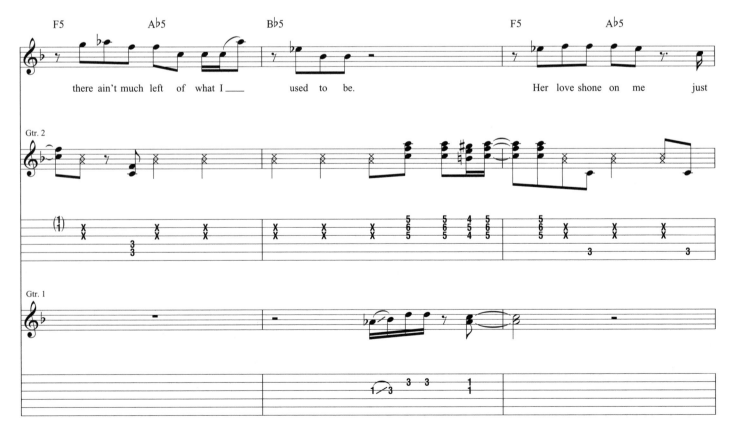

like the morn-ing light, ___ but now here I am, ___ a - lone a - gain __ to - night, _____

Chorus

Gtr. 1: w/ Rhy. Fig. 1 (1st 4 meas., 4 times)
Gtr. 2: w/ Rhy. Fig. 2

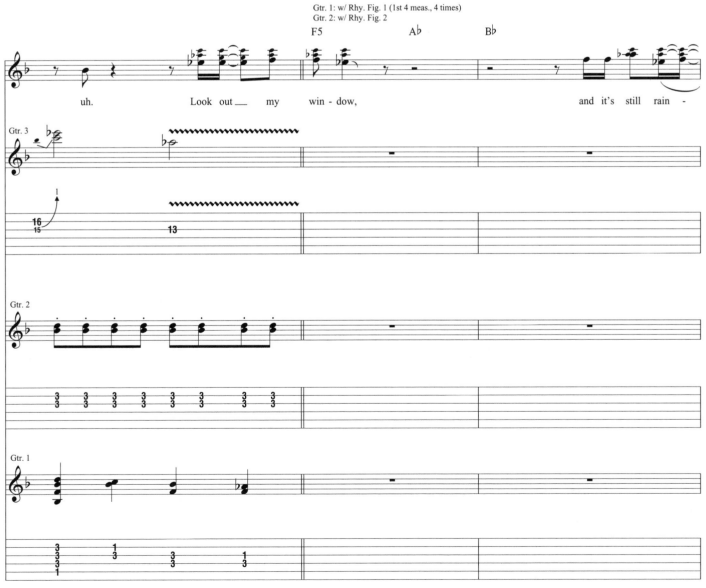

uh. Look out __ my win - dow, and it's still rain -

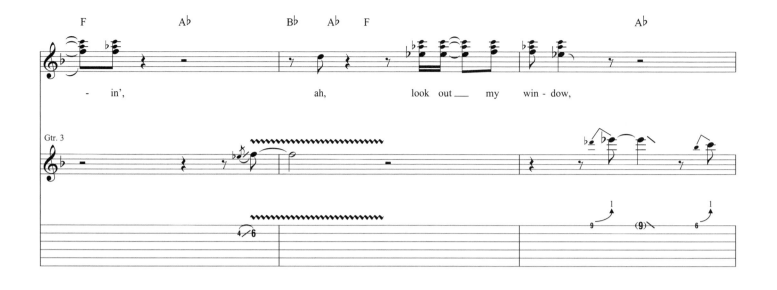

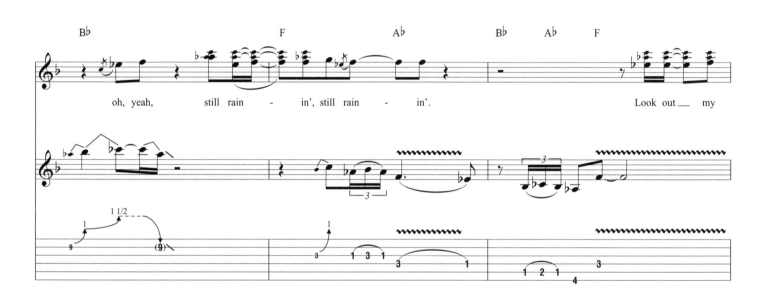

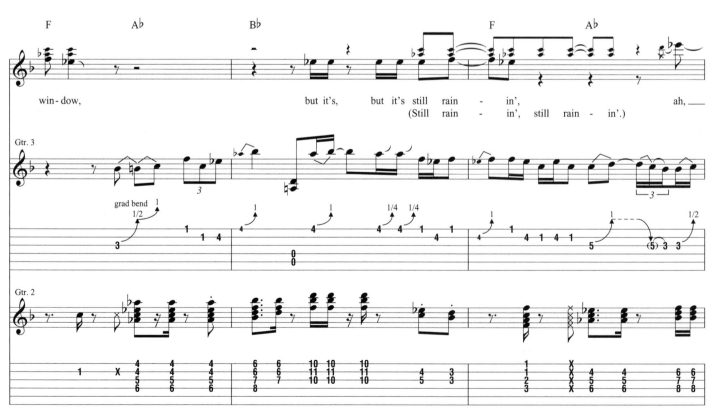

it's still,   it's still.
- in',   still rain - in',

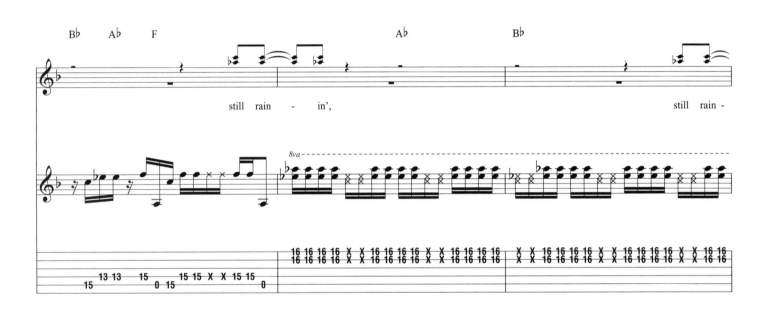

still rain - in',   still rain -

Fade out

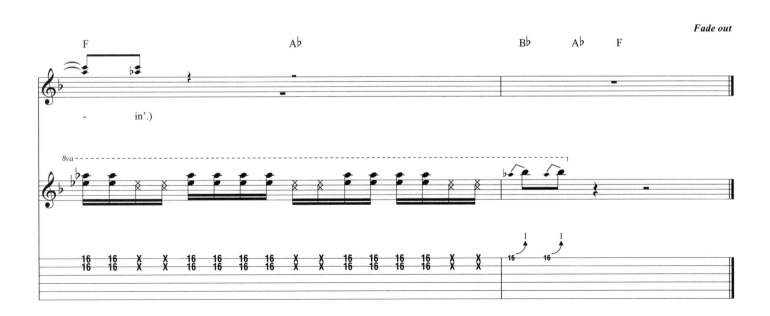

- in'.)

from T-Bone Walker - *The Very Best of*

Strollin' with Bones

Words and Music by T-Bone Walker, Vida Lee Walker and Edward Davis, Jr.

*Played as even eighth notes.

*Played as even eighth notes.

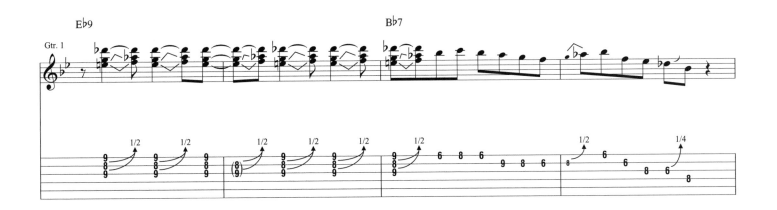

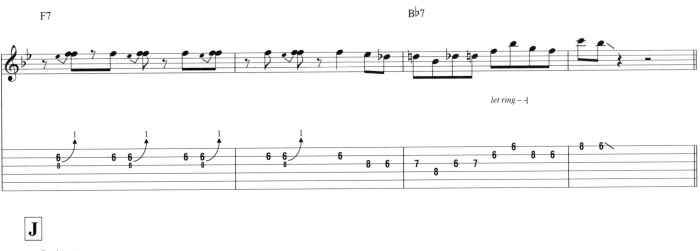

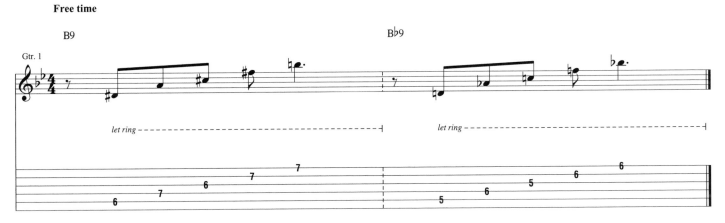

Sweet Sixteen

Words and Music by B.B. King and Joe Bihari

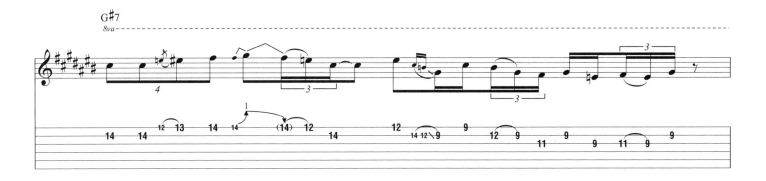

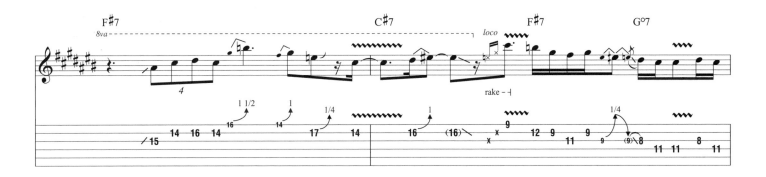

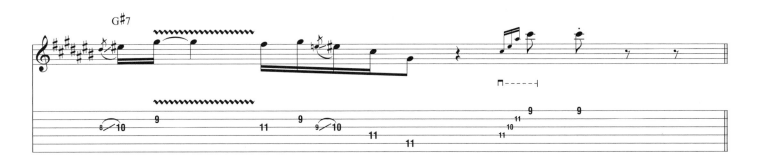

Verse

1. When I first met you, ba - by, baby, __

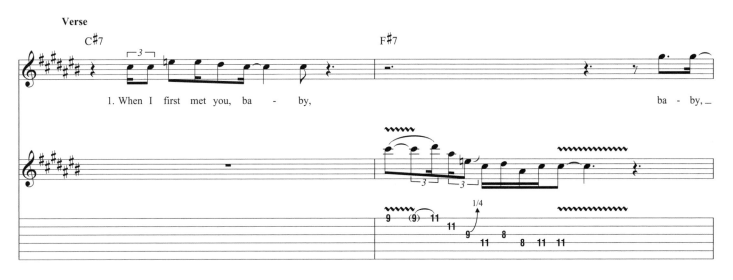

there ain't noth-ing, noth-ing in the world __ I would-n't do for you.

Guitar Solo

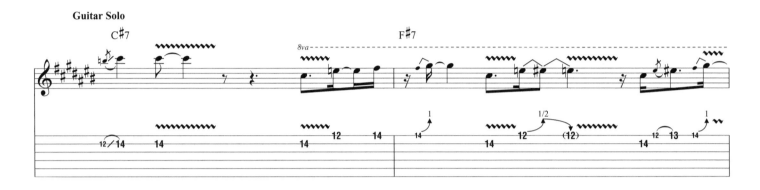

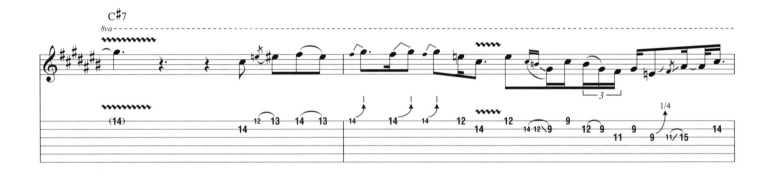

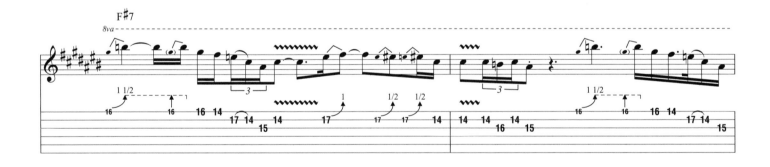

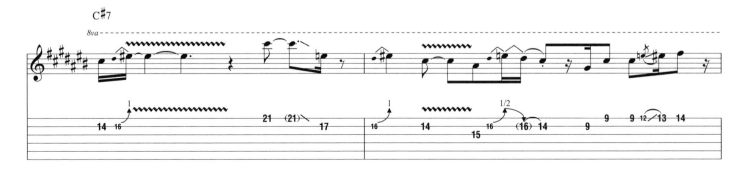

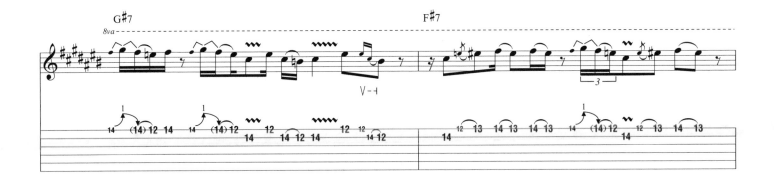

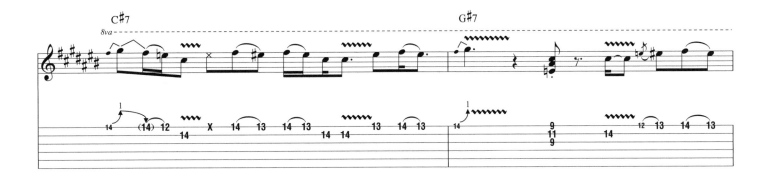

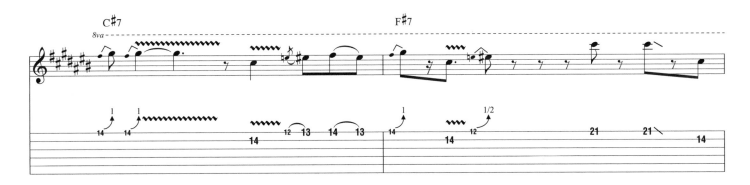

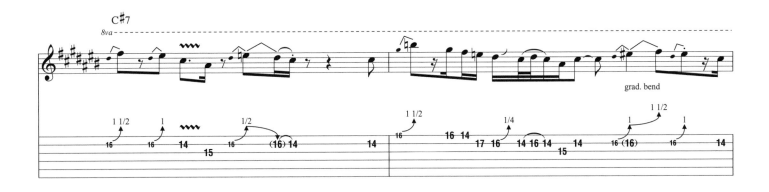

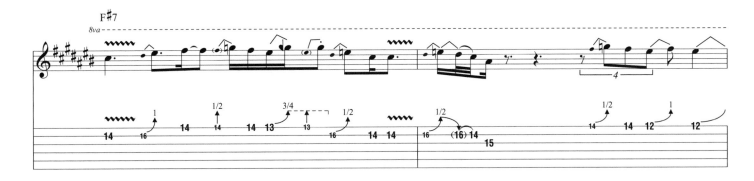

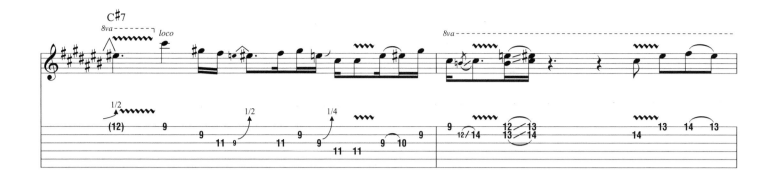

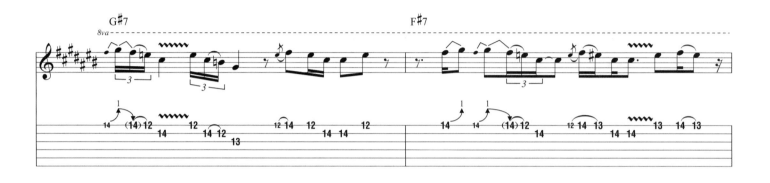

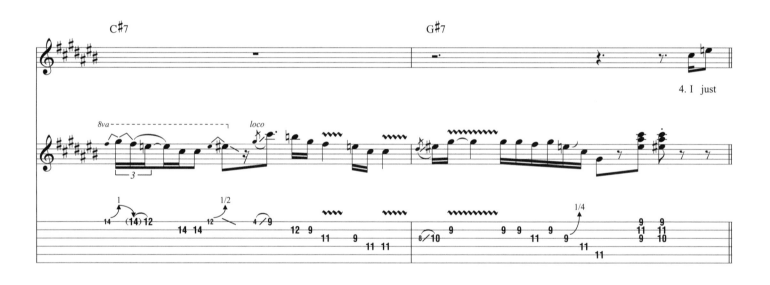

4. I just

Verse

got back from Vi - et - nam, __ ba - by,   and ya know I'm a long, long __

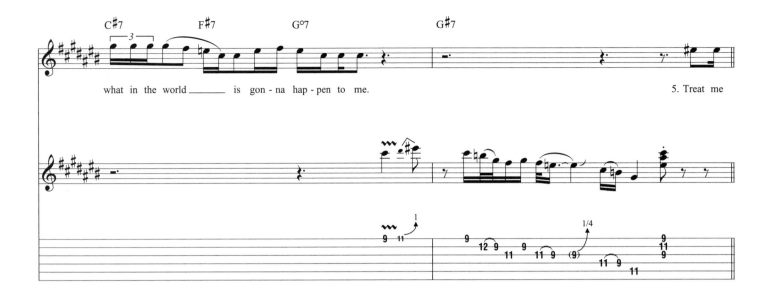

what in the world _____ is gon-na hap-pen to me.   5. Treat me

Verse

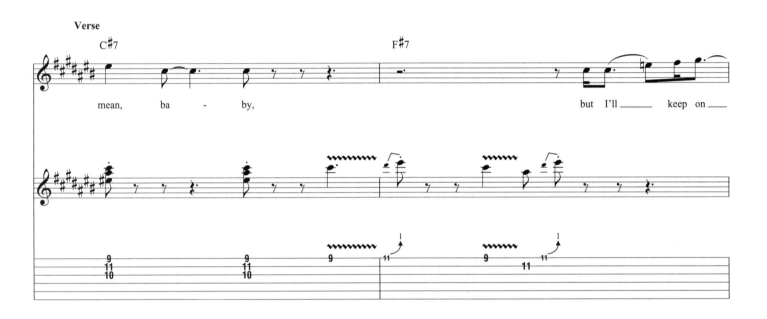

mean,   ba -   by,   but I'll _____   keep on _____

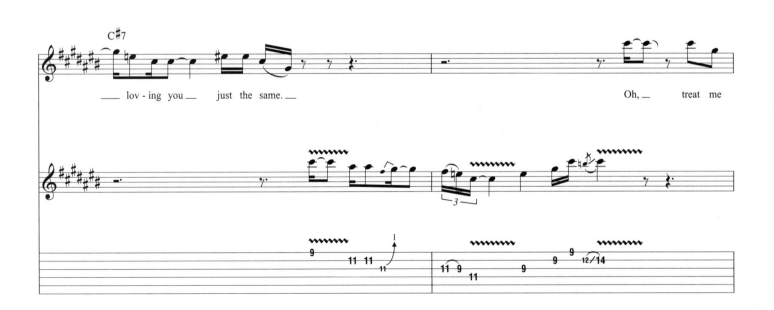

_____ lov-ing you _____ just the same. _____   Oh, _____   treat me

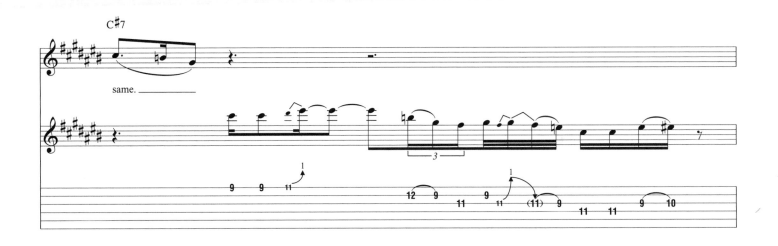

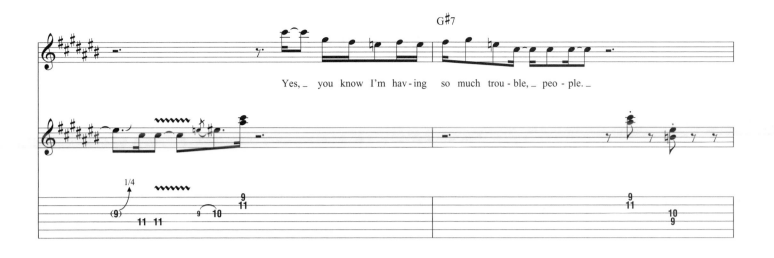

Yes, __ you know I'm hav-ing so much trou-ble, __ peo-ple. __

Free time

Gtr. tacet

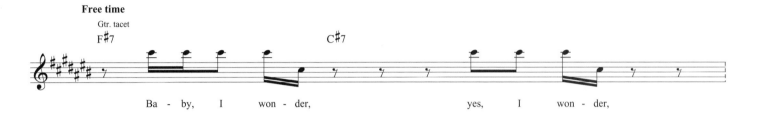

Ba - by, I won - der, yes, I won - der,

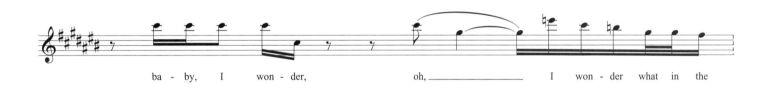

ba - by, I won - der, oh, _____ I won - der what in the

A tempo

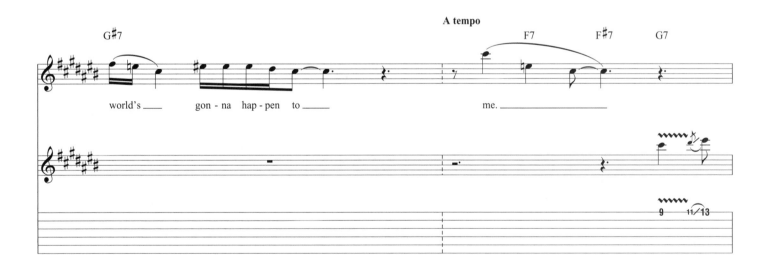

world's ___ gon - na hap - pen to ___ me. ___

Free time

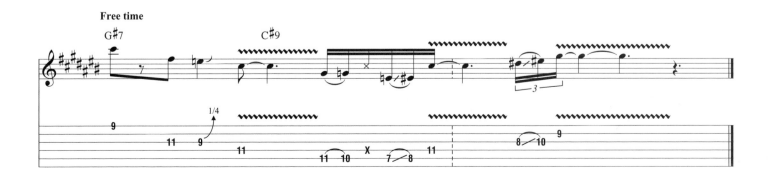

from Stevie Ray Vaughan and Double Trouble - *Texas Flood*

Texas Flood

Words and Music by Larry Davis and Joseph W. Scott

Tune down 1/2 step:
(low to high) E♭-A♭-D♭-G♭-B♭-E♭

Intro
Slow ♩. = 60

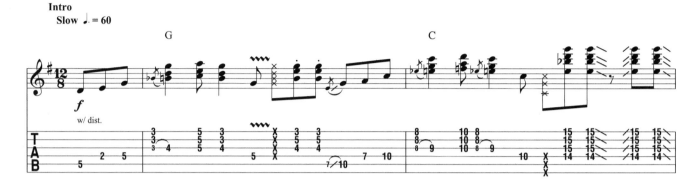

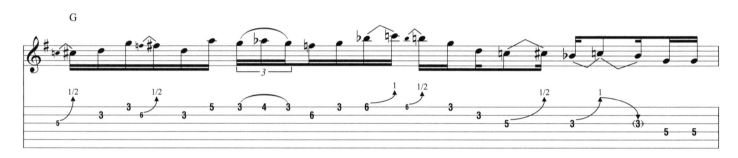

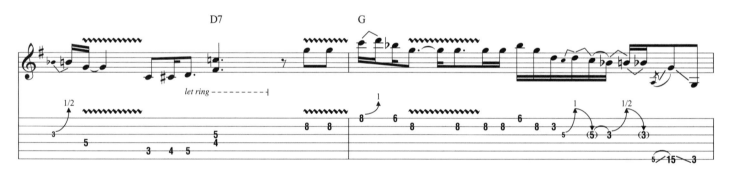

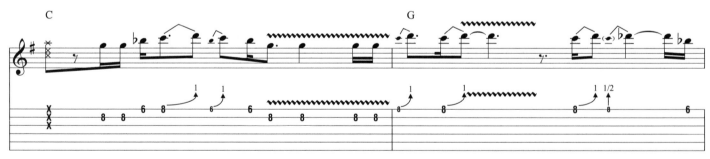

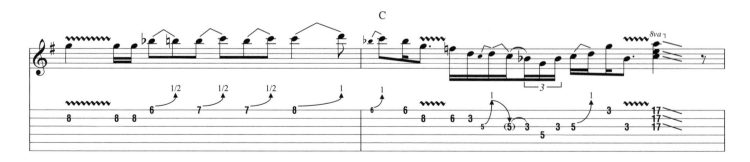

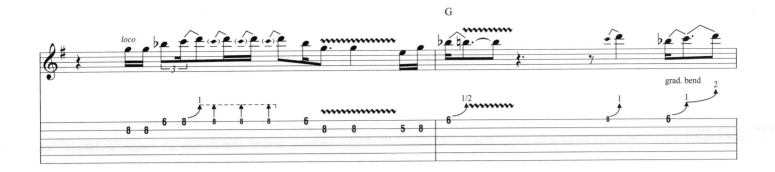

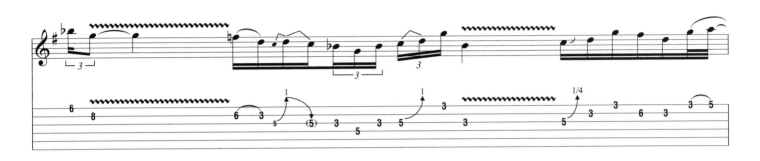

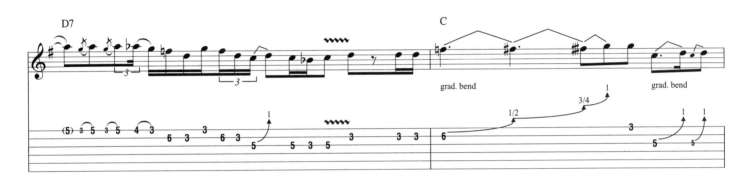

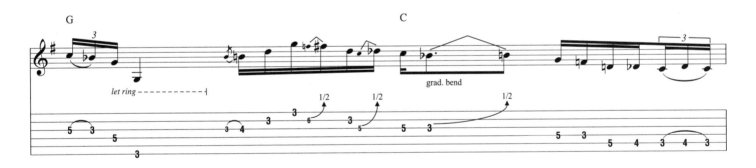

Verse

1. Well, __ it's flood-in' down in Tex-as. __

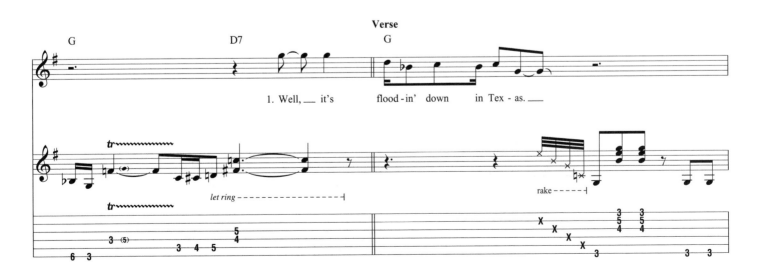

All of the tel-e-phone lines ___ are down. ___

Well, ___ it's ___

flood-in' down ___ in Tex-as. ___   All ___ of the tel-e-phone lines ___ are down. ___

Yeah, ___ I been

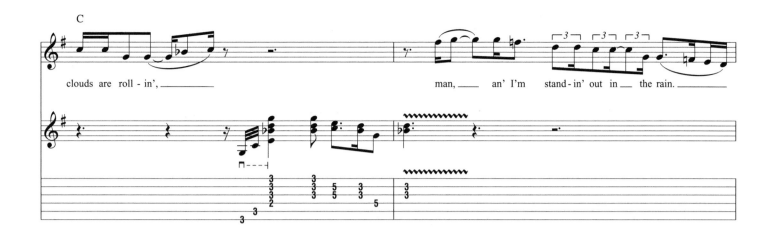

clouds are roll-in', _____ man, ___ an' I'm stand-in' out in ___ the rain. _____

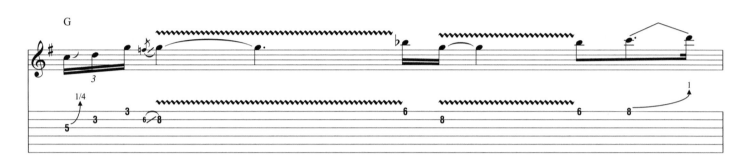

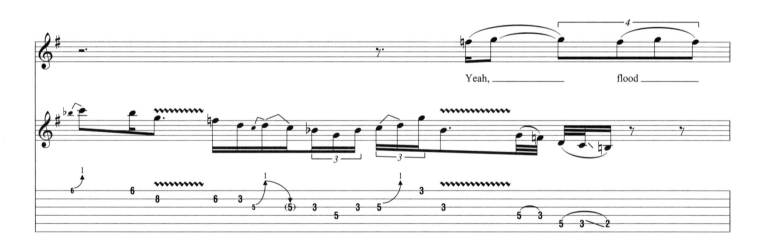

Yeah, _____ flood _____

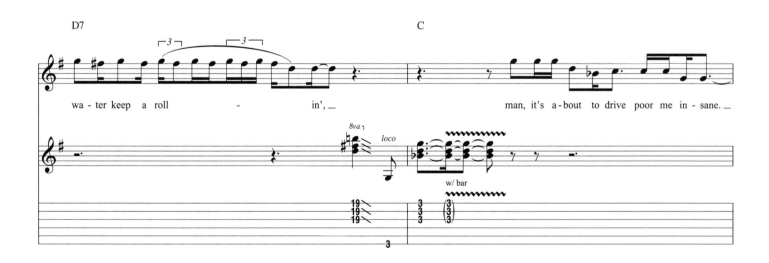

wa-ter keep a roll - in', ___ man, it's a-bout to drive poor me in - sane. ___

Guitar Solo

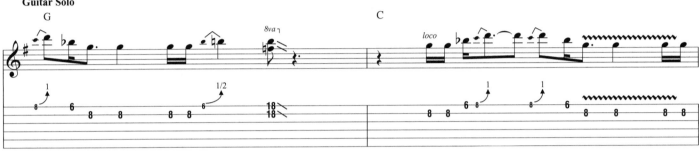

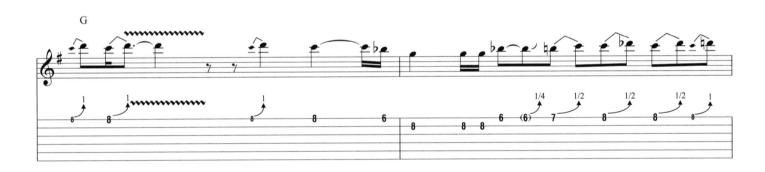

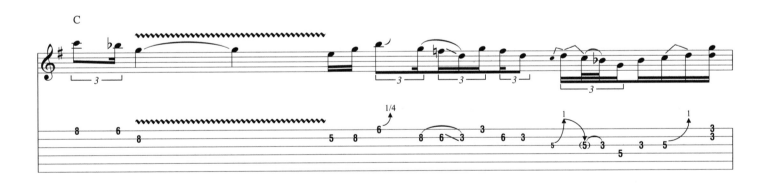

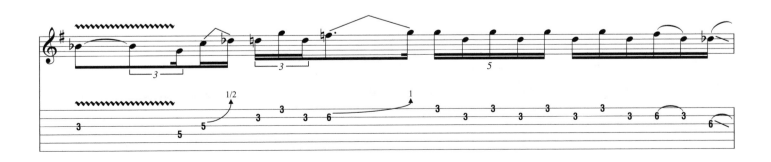

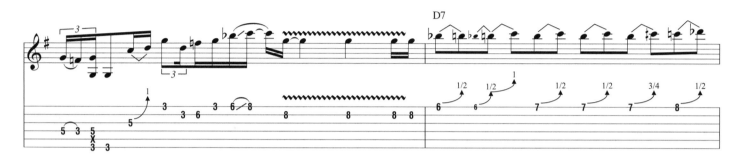

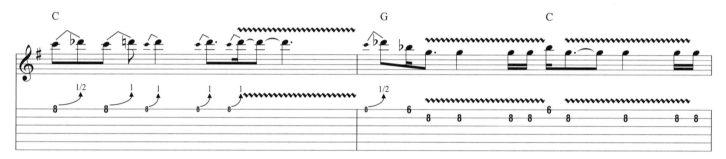

*Bend both strings w/ same finger, next 2 meas.

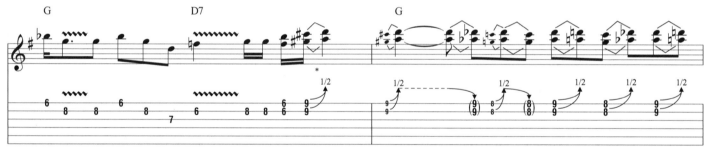

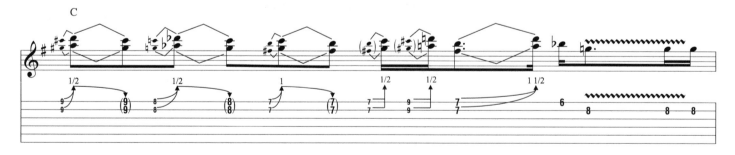

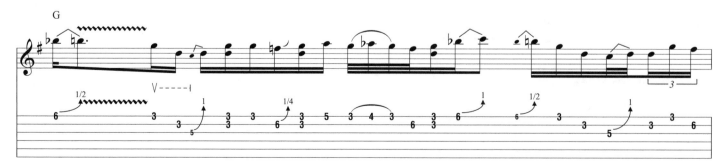

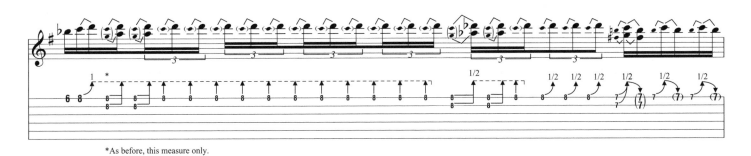

*As before, this measure only.

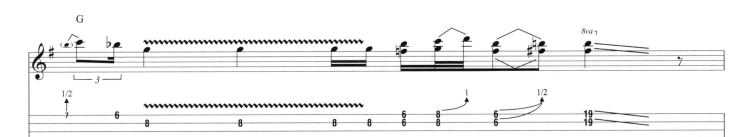

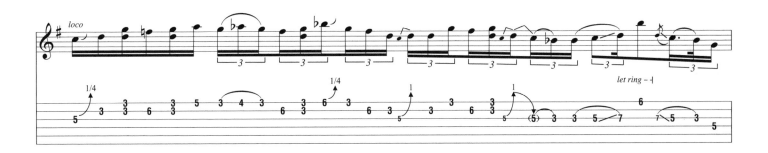

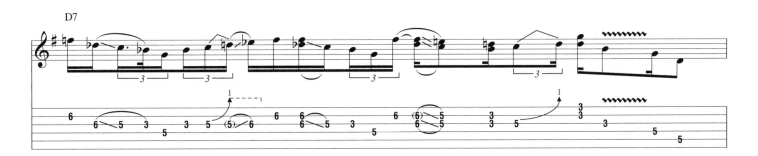

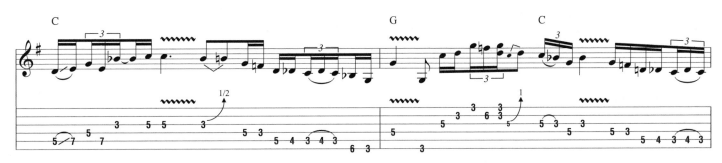

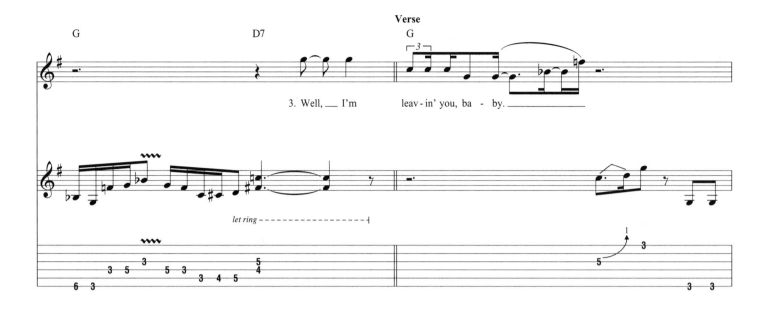

3. Well, __ I'm leav-in' you, ba - by. ____

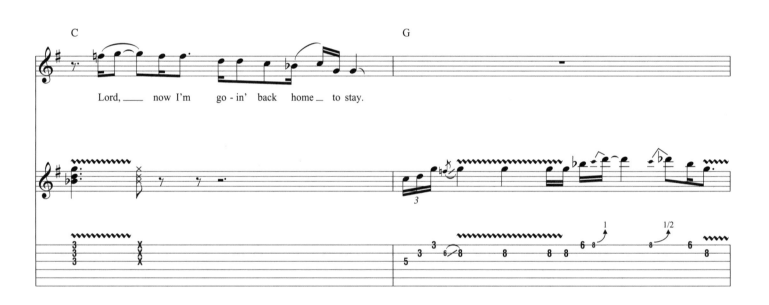

Lord, __ now I'm go - in' back home __ to stay.

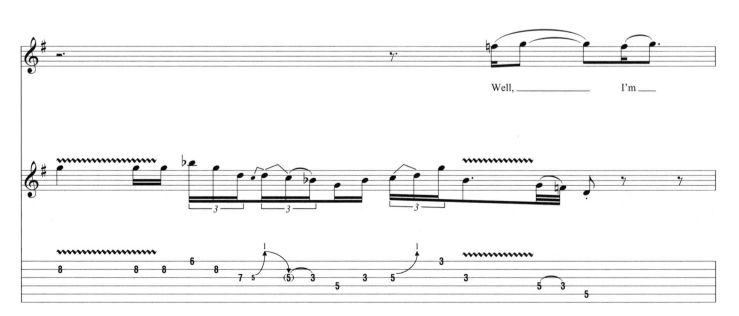

Well, _____ I'm ____

leav - in' you, ba - by. _____

Lord, _____ 'n' I'm go - in' back home to stay.

Well, __ back

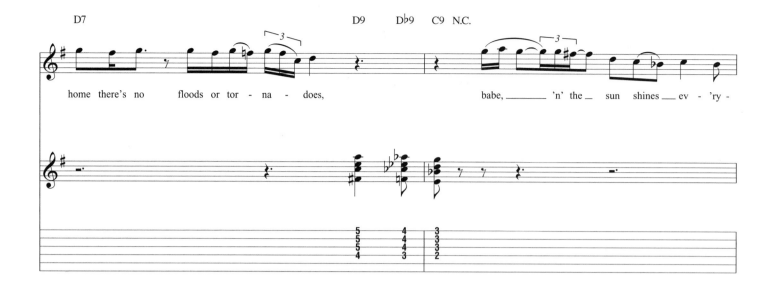

home there's no floods or tor - na - does, babe, ___ 'n' the ___ sun shines ___ ev - 'ry -

Free time

day. ___

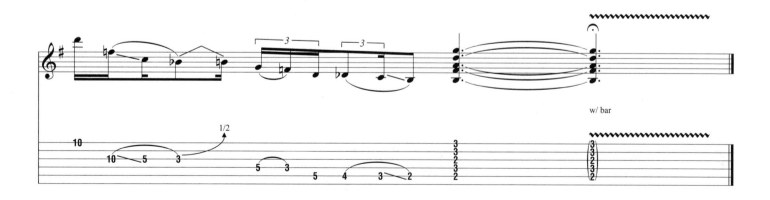

w/ bar